akiane
her life, her art, her poetry

akiane and foreli kramarik

THOMAS NELSON

Since 1798

NASHVILLE   DALLAS   MEXICO CITY   RIO DE JANEIRO

Published in Nashville, Tennessee by Thomas Nelson.
Thomas Nelson is a registered trademark of Thomas Nelson, Inc.

Thomas Nelson, Inc. titles may be purchased in bulk for educational, business, fund-raising, or
sales promotional use. For information, please e-mail SpecialMarkets@ThomasNelson.com.

Library of Congress Cataloging-in-Publication Data available

ISBN: 978-0-8499-0044-0

Printed in the United States of America
12 13 14 15 LBM 16 15 14 13 12

I DEDICATE THIS BOOK TO MY FATHER IN

HEAVEN AND HIS CREATION.

contents

AKIANE

akiane
her life

Akiane at 3 months old

The First Years

Two weeks overdue, but exactly on the destined due date, our daughter was born as a hot, muggy July day dawned over our home. Like millions of other parents, we felt that there had to be some Higher Power behind this wonder, but at the time we knew nothing about Him, nor did we suspect the spiritual transformation that our family would experience due to the influence of this nine-pound baby girl.

After her underwater birth, we held her in the warmth of the birthing pool as she looked up at us with her blue eyes. Through the ripples we could see her long hair floating in the water and her delicate fingers occasionally grasp the pulsing umbilical cord. My husband, Markus, cut the cord, and we named our newborn after the Russian word for "ocean": *Akiane*.

"She will have bright eyes," he noticed.

"She will be a picky eater!" I said as I observed the way she suckled.

Relieved that the home labor had passed without serious complications, we were elated to kiss and rock our third child. The midwife had come, but only to tell us we needed to pay her. And so it was that Akiane came into the world on her own.

We had recently moved from Chicago to the small town of Mount Morris, Illinois, and the only place we could afford was a shack on the edge of a cornfield. Outside of the house we felt no safety; one neighbor was murdered, another caused fire after fire

AKIANE

by burning trash next to our windows, another tried to shoot our dog, and another threatened to assault us if we didn't attend church. The interior of our house was unpleasant as well. The walls and flooring were cracked, moldy, and splattered with paint, and no matter how much we cleaned and scrubbed, the place was unsightly. We didn't have much furniture: one bed, one table, one chair, one rocker, and one empty bookshelf. There was no sink in the kitchen, so we washed the dishes in the bathroom or in the foul-smelling, flooded basement. But somehow none of this bothered us much, for we were busy talking, laughing, and playing. I was able to be with the children all the time, and they received my complete attention.

One day, while climbing the steep and crumbling concrete stairs outside our home, I tripped, and since there was no railing, fell. Three-week-old swaddled Akiane fell out of my arms and landed right on her face, straight onto the hard asphalt. The fall was terrible! I was sobbing along with my little baby, whose face began to swell and bleed profusely.

Akiane cried all day long. That evening we received a strange call from Europe telling us about a certain woman named Victoria, from the mountains of Armenia, who was telling many people about the incredible future of a girl named Akiane. A little later she called us herself and, with a thick Russian accent, tried to verbalize the spectacular events that were ahead for our daughter. Since she was a Christian and we were not believers, we did not take her passionate talk seriously, letting it go in one ear and out the other, completely rejecting it. Nevertheless, from that strange phone call we took the hope that our daughter would not be affected by the trauma of the fall that morning. Maybe that was all we needed to hear. The next day Akiane stopped crying, and her face began healing rapidly. After the incident we never again swaddled her but kept her close in a sling or a baby carrier.

With her frequent giggles and sunny personality, our newborn brought joy to all of us. She was very affectionate, sensitive, observant, and shy.

Our family led a fairly simple life; Markus commuted a long distance to work as a chef while I stayed home with Akiane and her two older brothers, Jeanlu, two, and Delfini, four. With little money and no friends nearby, we had to create our own fun. Every day I would dress our children warmly and take them across the cornfields to watch the sun set over the nuclear power plant that was visible on the horizon. We spent hours counting the birds in the sky and guessing which direction the steam from the plant would drift. At home we made a swing for Akiane, where she spent many

AKIANE

hours rocking and napping. The boys grew monarch butterflies from cocoons they found in the meadows, wrote their own books, and turned tree branches into swords. They made wreaths from flowers or pine needles, play-dough from flour, tents from blankets, and forts from cardboard boxes or snow.

The children and I made carrot pancakes and almond cookies to share with the neighbors, but although we knocked on doors to invite our neighbors over for tea or dinner, we realized that no one was interested in getting to know us. Almost every day we walked a few miles to the playground in hope of meeting playmates for the children—or anyone with whom we could share a conversation. But everyone seemed content with their own social circles.

Our daughter learned to crawl and walk very early, and after taking her first steps, she was very deliberate in every move, rarely falling down. The only delay in her development was talking, as she preferred to listen and would say only a few words. She always chose to observe new places and families from a safe distance before engaging in any direct interaction, and since the playground suited her personality, it soon became her favorite place to meet new faces, challenges, and adventures. Akiane liked to stay there half the day—even on chilly days—so we always packed books, blankets, and plenty of food.

My husband Markus's long work hours eventually wore him down. With severe asthma, his health began to deteriorate. When he took on a second job to help make ends meet, the combination of stress and asthma caused him to lose weight rapidly. Without money to see a doctor, he began to fear the worst. I would often hear him say, "I might not last long. Please, think now about how you—by yourself—could support our three children. There's no one to help us, and I am too weak . . . I don't know how much longer I can go on."

Akiane at 18 months old

Although I cherished my time with the children, because of the heavy burden of poverty and sickness in our family, I became involved in a sales business that, surprisingly, began to flourish very fast. At home, in the same room where our three little children played, I reluctantly learned about the outside world.

As a toddler, Akiane paid close attention to textures and fabrics. She loved to bring home rocks, shells, leaves, and flowers. When we went shopping or out to meet people, she insisted on touching each person's clothing and feeling the different textures of

AKIANE

skin. Since she was a very tactile child, we brought her a live bunny from a farm, and then a black Newfoundland puppy, which she loved feeding, training, and grooming. Her fascination with living creatures was apparent even then.

Akiane and her father

Akiane was unusually sensitive to the moods of those around her. She was quick to sense someone's essence, even through the thickest masks of laughter and smiles. "That woman is bad," she might observe—even if it was the exact opposite of what Markus and I had perceived. And if we left her with someone she didn't like for even a few minutes, she wouldn't stop crying until she was back safe in our laps. Surprisingly, her first impressions of people proved accurate time and time again.

By the time Akiane was two years old, my sales and advertising business had become so lucrative that we earned enough bonus money to purchase a house. I reached the top position in our nutritional product company, and after receiving an award and a sizable check, we packed our little white truck and drove from state to state looking for a new home.

We finally found a home in the state of Missouri, a ten-thousand-square-foot replica of a Frank Lloyd Wright house situated by a lake on a golf course, at an unbelievable bargain price. The children especially delighted in the new place. They often jumped off a trampoline into the twenty-foot diving end of our indoor pool, chased a cleaning robot, and warmed up in a sauna or a huge hot tub. They spent endless hours riding their bikes down the long hallways, fishing in the backyard, and playing hide-and-seek on the flat roof.

Our new financial situation also allowed us to buy fresh organic food, and our children were able to eat fruit as often as they liked. We frequently enjoyed lobster, freshly baked bread, avocado smoothies, and coconuts. We could also afford advanced medical care, but even this did not improve Markus's health, as the humidity in Missouri only exacerbated his asthmatic condition.

After a year, the thrill of the large house had died down, and we realized that we'd made a huge mistake. We just didn't need all of that space. In fact, we didn't even call it our home anymore; we jokingly called it "the Frank Lloyd *Wrong* house," "the sanatorium," "the Pentagon," or just "the hotel." And so we resolved to hire a Realtor and

AKIANE

put it up for sale. With shoes neatly lined up by the door, with towels perfumed in the bathrooms, with the slate black tile floor polished to perfection, we had one showing after another—but no one was interested.

Dreams and Drawings Begin

Akiane at age 3

Before we could fully comprehend what was happening, I found myself in the sinkhole of the business world. Although Markus helped me with office duties every day and I was able to work mostly from home, I felt that over time my bond with my children had been weakened. I was pulled between the business and the family. Money didn't seem to bring us more happiness; instead, my work was clouding the joy of motherhood that I had once experienced.

Because Akiane and her brothers had only a few acquaintances and had never formed deep relationships with anyone outside the family, they played mostly with one another. Our family never talked about religion, never prayed together, and never went to any church. I had been raised as an atheist in Lithuania, and Markus had been raised in an environment not conducive to spiritual growth. The children did not watch television, had never been out of our sight, and were homeschooled; therefore, we were certain that no one else could have influenced Akiane's sudden and detailed descriptions of an invisible realm. We can't remember the exact month, but one morning when Akiane was four, she began sharing her visions of heaven with us.

"Today I met God," Akiane whispered to me one morning.

"What is God?" I was surprised to hear this. To me, God's name always sounded absurd and primitive.

"God is light—warm and good. It knows everything and talks with me. It is my parent."

"Tell me more about your dream."

"It was not a dream. It was real!"

I looked at her slightly puffed eyes, and in complete disbelief I kept on asking her questions. "So who is your God?"

"I cannot tell you." Akiane lowered her head.

"Me? You cannot tell your own mom?"

"The Light told me not to." She was firm.

"Akiane, darling, you can share anything with me. You know I won't tell anyone."

"Yes, you will. You cannot know."

"Why did you think it was God?"

"Just like I know you are my mommy, and you know I am Akiane."

"Who even taught you such a word *God*?"

"You won't understand."

I was astonished to think she felt she could not tell her own mother. Even more puzzling was the fact that she had learned the word *God* on her own. Upset and uncomfortable, I suggested that maybe it was a nightmare and that if she would just talk to me, I could help.

I begged her that whole day to tell me anything at all about her dream, but she

Foreli and Akiane in front of their home

never gave in. About six weeks passed before I succeeded, finally reaching a point where she would describe to me details about life with God and the future of the earth. We no longer suspected she was imagining such events, because she had never fantasized like other children her age. She never initiated pretend games, talked with imaginary friends, or visualized living in other places as so many young girls do. With her matter-of-fact approach to life, she always took play and work very seriously, preferring everything to be real. She simply had no interest in fairy tales, fantasies, or anything artificial.

Now she began to share these new experiences, which were unlike anything we were accustomed to hearing. The smallest details, the prophetic speech, and the sense that she spent more time away in the spiritual world than with our family were all hard to ignore. Sometimes she sounded like an older woman—not because of her voice, but because of her total sincerity, her strangely compelling comments, and her broad vocabulary. It scared us and inspired us at the same time.

Though I had promised I would not tell anyone, I did not keep my promise to her. Since I burned to share her stories with others, somehow, little by little, I started relat-

AKIANE

ing them to a lot of people. I was giving away Akiane's secrets. But it was premature; what Akiane knew and saw was not meant to be known or disclosed, for neither I nor others were able to handle the messages at that time. I learned when Akiane shared these dreams and visions, which to her were actual life experiences, to stop telling others. I simply began recording them in a journal.

About the same time as the visions began, Akiane suddenly began showing an intense interest in drawing. She began sketching hundreds of figures and portraits on whatever surfaces she found at hand, including walls, windows, furniture, books, and even her own legs and arms. The different poses were drawn mostly from her imagination. Sometimes she scribbled and sketched with her eyes closed, and sometimes with her pencil between her toes or her teeth. There were also times when I would find our white walls smeared with charcoal from our fireplace or with fruits and vegetables from the garden. And sometimes after a reprimand she would scribble on the bottom of the tables so we would not see her mischief.

Akiane's angel, drawn at the age of 4

One day we noticed white spots on her front teeth. We asked what had happened, but Akiane just turned away.

"Akiane ate a tube of toothpaste," Delfini accused. "Her angel's teeth are so white, they sparkle. She thought that if she ate toothpaste, her teeth would also get whiter."

The next morning, after unscrewing almost the entire bookshelf to make an easel, Akiane woke me up at 4:00 a.m. by waving a drawing of a woman over my face. "Look! This is her—this is my angel," Akiane explained. "Her skin is so smooth, not one spot. She doesn't smile in my picture, because paper is not white enough to show how white her teeth are, and I wanted to show how she talks to me with her eyes. You see, where God takes me, He teaches me how to draw."

Our four-year-old daughter was most inspired by faces, and she would sit for hours drawing, erasing, and shading their features. For the next two years, the walls of our home were filled with sketches of her family, her acquaintances, and faces that she dreamed about. At this point she didn't work with colors; she asked only for lead pencils and charcoal.

Akiane seemed unusually patient and serious for one so young, totally dedicated to her work. Not a perfectionist in any other area of her life, this intensity of focus came as a surprise to us. She'd leave her room untidy or her hair uncombed, but her portraits always had to be absolutely perfect.

Her images were often very perceptive. Once, when Akiane sketched the portrait of a woman who seemed to be very happy, she depicted her subject with a very sad expression. Upon seeing the picture, the woman tearfully admitted that her happiness was a front, for she had just lost her only son. Another day she showed me a sketch of myself looking to the side. "You look away from me and my brothers! I want to be with you more . . . You spend all your time in your office and have no time to play chess with me. We need each other. We need kisses."

"My Mother," drawn at age 4

One summer afternoon Akiane ran around the house feeling all the glass, tiles, stones, and walls that she could get her hands on. After being unable to find any material that matched what she wanted to describe, she sat quite disappointed on the tile floor and started sketching a series of concentric circles with a candle on the pool window. "Oh, no, I can't find it here. I can't show you the house of Light. I wish you could see it. It's so beautiful and so big! It looks like circle, circle, circle, circle inside circle, circle, and circle . . . God lives there. Walls like glass, but not glass. Water pink, purple, and many other colors I can't find here. Trees and grass are not green there. There are . . ." She ran outside and promptly returned with a fuchsia flower. "Close to this color. Then I plant a tree, a big tree. It has yummy fruit."

"What fruit?"

"It tastes good, better than anything you've ever tasted. The Light gives me fruit."

"For what?"

"To breathe."

"What do you mean?"

"To live. I plant that big tree. You will eat it too."

"Why me?"

"I don't know. God says many will need to eat that. The tree will always be there on a new earth."

AKIANE

"What else do you remember?"

"I eat there, but I don't go to the bathroom. The plants there move and sing when I move and talk. It seems as if they can think. Animals there are not like here. They listen to me, and they're not afraid of me, so I can pet them whenever I want. Some of them create the most amazing plant sculptures. I also fly on top of huge birds there while I am strapped inside a cage that looks like this." She touched a diamond inside my wedding ring. "I am good there, and I listen there. Everyone listens there—God is there."

Slowly and cautiously, Markus and I tried to logically fathom the realm our daughter was sharing with us, but we just couldn't do it. We had to either take a leap of faith or remain locked up in skepticism and doubt. The leap was not a step and not a climb—it was a direct fall. We didn't know what was below, but we had a hunch that it wasn't worse than where we were standing. For the first time, we began sharing with each other our own budding faith. After several discussions, both of us came to the conclusion that it was better to believe in God and to be wrong than to believe that there was no God and to be right. The way we thought about it, we had nothing to lose by believing.

When Akiane was four and a half she started showing great interest and talent in gymnastics, but when she found out that all professional gymnasts suffered through quite a few injuries throughout their careers, she had to make the difficult decision

AKIANE'S DRAWINGS AT AGE 4

between art and gymnastics. After giving this plenty of thought, she chose healthy hands for her art.

Then she started dancing. She danced on the couches, on chairs, and in bathtubs. She danced in front of a mirror and in front of our family and guests. Greatly intrigued by movement, physiology, and anatomy, our daughter was now inspired to be a ballerina and a doctor. Anything relating to health, the human body, or behavior simply intrigued her.

But there were few things harder to understand than Akiane's response to music. For her first five years, she would start to cry every time any kind of music was played. Later, when she was able to talk, she would beg us to stop the music—and no one had the slightest idea why. One evening after another similar confrontation, I broke down. I simply couldn't understand her. As I sobbed, I felt small hands raise my wet face, and I barely heard my five-year-old's apology.

"Mommy, please, please, don't cry. I'm sorry I act this way, but the music that I hear in heaven is better than here. This music hurts my ears and my head really bad, but heavenly music is always gentle. I can't tell you how different it is from what you hear on earth! It feels like joy, looks like love, smells like flowers, and dances like butterflies. Music there is alive! You can even taste it."

More and more, Markus and I were confronted with Akiane's independent thinking, so we took steps to understand her and her faith. Our embryonic perception of

AKIANE'S DRAWINGS AT AGE 5

AKIANE

Akiane, age 5, and her mother

Divinity, however, was still very frail, and during any hardship we would slip back to our own tangible and logical world full of proofs and questioning. We could marvel at Akiane's faith, but we had to start somewhere for ourselves. Inspired by her spirituality, and for the first time ever, Markus took the family to visit a few different churches. But what we found seemed to be a place for adults and not children.

As we continued to assemble the Akiane puzzle, we decided that I should quit my job and once again devote my attention to our children full-time. Unfortunately, after I resigned, Markus couldn't find a decent job for a number of months. Our huge home had been on the market for a long time already, and soon we began living as if we were in a hotel without occupants, draining our entire investment.

"We need to stay here longer. When it's time, we will sell." Akiane tried to comfort us with each passing month, but our financial troubles were growing. We had to sell our furniture, the car, the playgrounds, and our library of books. Akiane was able to bring in a small amount of money by teaching other children to draw, but our family continued accumulating heavy debts just to stay afloat. It

AKIANE'S DRAWINGS AT AGE 5

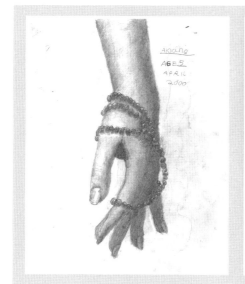

seemed so odd that we owned one of the largest and most famous residential houses in the county, but we drove an old, rusty pickup truck, ate canned beans, washed our clothes by hand, dusted empty bookshelves, and cooked potatoes in the fireplace.

Yet at this point, because of our newfound belief, we were even more drawn to God. For the first time in our lives, we were experiencing indescribable joy, harmony, and peace.

A New World of Color and Words

Despite our financial plight, God impressed upon us to have a fourth child—a decision that led to the most difficult pregnancy I had ever experienced. I was confined to my bed and suffered severe, round-the-clock vomiting, and if I had to leave the house, it was always with the aid of my husband and a wheelchair. Because of the challenges we faced during this time, we felt that we could no longer school the children properly ourselves. We assumed that a religious school would be most suitable for our daughter's spiritual inclinations, so we sent the children to a parochial school that, due to our circumstances, offered us free tuition. Although Akiane enjoyed the structure, the studies, and the friends she'd made in her first-grade class, she

Brother Jeanlu and Akiane, age 6

often complained about the noise. By the time she finished her classes and came home for the day, she was inclined to rest and had very little energy left for art.

As busy and sick as Markus and I both were, we gradually began to recognize Akiane's unique talents. We had more questions than answers about her dreams, though at that time we were only comfortable sharing with others her unusual gift for art. One day at the craft store, Akiane

Akiane at age 6

AKIANE

spotted a box of oil pastels. Although she'd never seen or touched any before, she announced, "I think I am ready to paint in color." At home she immediately began to explore the new medium that we had purchased for her, rubbing her fingers between the sticks to blend them. The world of color was now wide open for her, and the more she worked with it, the more confident and joyful she became.

On one occasion, Markus and I asked Akiane and her friends to participate in a county art competition. She was the youngest contestant and didn't even win a ribbon. The jury simply told us she had no talent. We tried to support Akiane by displaying her drawings at local art and craft fairs, only to be disappointed again. Most people doubted that a six-year-old could be so artistically advanced; they refused to believe our daughter had actually created the pictures.

Akiane, brother Delfini, and mother at a local art show

"Mommy, how come no one looks at my drawings?" Akiane asked me sadly during her first show. "Look, the teachers of my school have just passed. I saw a librarian and the banker. Have you seen how they looked at our stand?"

"How?"

"Without any 'wow.' Without any interest . . ."

Barely attached to the display wall with pushpins, Akiane's drawings were flapping in the wind. We couldn't afford frames.

"Akiane, I just don't know why their eyes aren't on your art."

"One day . . . one day it will be different, Mama. One day it will change."

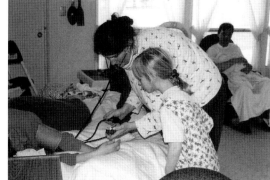

That spring, in the same inflatable pool we had used for all the underwater births, we had an eleven-pound boy. The minute Ilia was born, the vinyl pool burst, as if to signal that this would be our last delivery. All three children were in the family room at the time of the birth, so immediately following

Akiane attending to her mother after her brother Ilia's birth

Ilia's arrival, they poured into the master bedroom. In no time, they were able to hold the plump newborn. Now that Akiane was no longer the youngest, her mannerisms and intonations seemed to instantly mature.

A few months before the school year ended, our family was on the brink of declaring bankruptcy. Since Realtors hadn't been able to sell the house in almost four years, even at a significantly reduced price, Akiane suggested that we try to sell the house ourselves. We felt we had nothing to lose. Surprisingly, we were able to find a buyer the very next day. Then almost immediately, Markus found a job in Boulder, Colorado, and we found ourselves moving into a brick house on the slope of a mountain.

Seven-year-old Akiane began attending second grade at a small mountain school. Unhappy about her studies and her high-altitude headaches, she begged us to take her out of public school and to move somewhere else. That year proved to be a disastrous year for the entire family—Mark and I were very sick; my parents, who lived in Europe, nearly died; Delfini was scalded by boiling water and airlifted by a helicopter to a Denver hospital; Jeanlu injured his leg; and Akiane's finger was accidentally severed by a closing door and then sewn back on. While we were dealing with one accident after another, Ilia, the baby, was developing a life-threatening autoimmune disease that caused him to become severely allergic to everything he ate, touched, or breathed, with open, deep, oozing sores all over his body that bled every day. Between the ambulance rides and nursing a sickly baby, it seemed as if the plague of worries would never leave us.

Although the children attended public school, I gave them the assignment of composing a few poems, a Christmas tradition from my home country.

"It's finished!" After a few days had passed, Akiane was the last of our children to put her handwritten poem on my lap. "But why do we have to have homeschool assignments after we come from school? It's so tiring!"

I couldn't read a word. Everything looked totally illegible and messy, so I had to ask her to read it to me. Even she could barely read her own writing, and with so many other things on my mind, I just couldn't focus on what she was reading. In order to understand the poem, I decided to write down what she was saying. Still, with our one-year-old son crying and babbling, I didn't give much attention to what she was dictating. After I changed a diaper, I grabbed the crumpled sheet of paper on which I'd written and finally focused on Akiane's poem. As I thumbed through it, scrambled with both Lithuanian and English words, I was flabbergasted.

AKIANE

Searching for Rainbows

Blind secrets feel the frozen bells
Whistling through the caves
To become heroes in God's army
Have we stood up like caged-up slaves

Harps burn like prisoners in brimstones
The sunset closed the garden gates
The razor jealousy has splintered promises
The foot traps locked our mistakes

We leave thirsty from the lifeless feasts
While royal crowns collect the dust
The empty hours steal the sweat of time
When we believe—who heals our trust

If we smell the love—spring follows the pain
Hard clay gets broken by the soft prayer
The bitter berries wilderness has planted
Somewhere the child awaits for us to share

Will the manure be found in paradise
We wish somehow to reach the answers
Heavy curtains fall to open our faith
The end gets lost—we touch all dances

Like color-blind ospreys searching for rainbows
We search for divine strength alone
Covered with wasps we walk in God's shadow
If we die with the smile—we journey home

Having put Ilia down for his nap, I rushed to the bathroom where Akiane was singing off-key in the shower. "How did you do it?"

"It just came to me!" Akiane answered with a mouthful of water.

"What do you mean it just came to you? Did you copy it from anywhere?"

"No!"

"Wait, wait . . . did you memorize it from anywhere?" And then I stopped there, remembering how difficult it was for her to memorize anything. More than once I had quit teaching her Russian simply because she could not remember new words.

"Mom!" She opened the shower curtain. "I promise, I wrote it on my own. You can ask Delfini. He saw me writing."

"I believe you . . . It just sounds too amazing to believe. You're a seven-year-old, not a seventy-year-old. What is your poem about?"

"Aha! You have to figure that out by yourself."

"What do you mean?"

"Well, if I told you what I wrote, there would be no mystery or adventure."

"So, tell me from the very beginning how you created it."

"Honestly?"

"Honestly."

"Well, I really had no ideas for a few days. But then I prayed, and all of a sudden I started seeing the words and images right inside my head. It's weird, but it happened. Honestly, I don't even know the meaning."

"Do you think it can happen again?"

"I don't know."

As I was rereading her thought-provoking poem, I started to sob. Her composition astonished us, especially knowing that Akiane always had quite a challenging time with languages. She was not articulate and didn't enjoy reading at all.

Akiane now began to either handwrite poetry or dictate it to me, often creating a poem effortlessly within seconds—a poem that needed no editing. Each poem seemed as dynamic and flawless as the next. There was no trance or automatic writing involved— we had no idea how she did it. We did know, however, that it was happening consistently every week.

Up until that time Akiane had read only nursery rhymes, so the source of the stunning imagery, rhythm, and aphoristic wisdom in her poetry was a mystery to us. We

AKIANE

observed her working and witnessed the evidence of her spirituality, but we could only guess and wonder at her intricate connection to the Spirit.

Strangely enough, she never spoke of her poems. At least at the beginning, writing was something she was totally indifferent about. It was like combing her hair—something she needed to do, but it wasn't of great importance to her. With the passing of time, Akiane felt more and more compelled to write, remaining completely oblivious to the maturity of her compositions. Often she would include words in her poetry that neither Markus nor I knew the meaning of. Some of her words, as it turned out, weren't in dictionaries, because they were combinations or composites of words that created new meanings.

Interestingly enough, Akiane was never drawn to read the works of other writers. "It's not time yet," she would remark whenever we offered to buy her a book of poetry. Even when we did buy her a few books, they only collected dust on the bookshelf.

Akiane's initial compositions were written in a combination of Lithuanian, English, and Russian. She would either scribble the poems down and fly them to me folded into paper airplanes, or urgently dictate them to me. After Akiane created a poem, she would undertake the process of translation, irritated that the translation would take her many times longer than the original writing. What she loved about poetry was that she could so quickly and effortlessly express ideas she didn't have to discuss—ideas that nobody judged. The process of translation, however, she regarded as an intrusion into her writing freedom. She found it tedious and time-consuming, and she worried that the specific meaning she sought to express would be changed as a result.

Soon Akiane was drawn to write only in English. Now that she felt free to record the ideas spontaneously without any need for translation, her interest in writing increased. Apparently many of the poems she wrote were connected; each poem seemed to explain or respond to another, as though they were all pieces in one great and complex jigsaw puzzle. Akiane herself noted that the messages were somehow coded. It was apparent that there was much more there than the eye could see or the ear could hear.

As her interest in poetry blossomed, her interest in schoolwork faded. Not a day passed without Akiane, who was now in second grade, asking us to take her out of school. "Let me study at home. Then I'd have time and energy to do art and poetry. After school I feel drained and have no inspiration to paint. And it's so noisy at school."

"You still get good grades. Aren't you one of the best students?" I searched for a good excuse for sending the children to school, but the real reason was that I had no idea how to homeschool all four children.

"Grades don't mean anything if I'm not interested. What's the meaning of all these studies if I can't help others? When half of the world goes to sleep hungry, what am I doing reading all those books?"

But it wasn't just words Akiane was exploring. Before long she was asking for real paints, because she had become bored and frustrated with oil pastels and their inability to render fine details.

Akiane (far right), age 7, on a school field trip

That Christmas the boys received a golden retriever puppy, and Akiane received her first set of acrylic paints. Right away she began working on her first painting, and for the next few days we barely caught even a glimpse of her.

When I peeked into her room one weekend, the whole blue shag carpet was covered with paint. The bedspread, the walls, her socks—almost everything was smeared with paint. I closed the door, took a deep breath, and reentered, but this time my eyes drifted to a Colorado winter landscape resting on her squeaky easel. Akiane was washing her brush in the amber-decorated jar that evidently was taken from my souvenir box without permission. For the longest time she assumed that if we loved one another we must share all the things we have. It was very difficult for her to distinguish her own belongings from the property of others. Since she didn't mind giving away her own possessions, it seemed fair to her that she could take something she needed from others without asking. According to her experiences in heaven, most things were shared.

These real paints seemed so different and magical to Akiane. Although she had quickly figured out how to mix and blend them, it took her a long time to figure out how to keep the paints off her body and every surface in her room. Her paint-stained clothes gave away her passion wherever she went.

After the winter holidays, Markus was unexpectedly laid off. As he struggled to find another job, we once again found ourselves seeking direction. And for the first time we felt the need to have our family pray together. It wasn't long before we were packing up to move again, this time to Idaho.

Artistic Marathons

Northern Idaho was one of the most idyllic places we had ever seen. Living close to a lake and to nature, and finally able to stay home and learn on her own, Akiane was inspired to paint and write every day. She was physically, emotionally, and spiritually revived. We also lived by a park, and our children often invited the neighbors over to play soccer or tennis. Soon they made new friends and spent hours frolicking and playing. There were so many youngsters left alone while their parents worked that we sometimes stuffed our small truck with children and drove to the city beach. Our kids felt that the neighborhood friends were better off swimming with them than watching television all day long. At the beach the youngsters would wrestle, sprint, play freeze-tag, build sand castles and tunnels, bury one another in the sand, snorkel, jump off the docks, or just lie in the sun and relax.

Akiane loved the lake and her new friends, but more than anything, she loved spending time with God and thinking about how she could help the whole world. This was also the time she became even more interested in writing.

Very early one morning, we found eight-year-old Akiane gazing through the window at the sky, her calm face glowing. When we asked what she was doing, she answered simply, "I was with God again, and I was told to pray continually. He showed me where He lived, and it was so light. He was whiter than the whitest of whites. I was climbing transparent stairs; underneath I saw gushing waterfalls. As I approached my Father in paradise, His body was pure light. What impressed me the most were His gigantic hands—they were full of maps and events. Then He told me to memorize thousands upon thousands of wisdom words on a scroll that didn't look like paper, but more like intense light. And in a few seconds I somehow got filled up. He showed me the endless universe, its past and its future, and He told me that from now on I needed to get up very early and get ready for my mission. I hope one day I'll be able to paint what I've been shown."

"What mission?" I couldn't help asking.

"You cannot understand that mission now, Mom. When that time comes, you will see."

She talked like this for quite some time, and as I listened, I was overwhelmed by the existence of the spiritual insights that were deeply impressing themselves on my own searching mind. The next day Akiane wrote a very long poem.

Conversation with God

I receive an envelope with the seal of Your lips
As I am waiting for You I get covered with dust
My heavy rope is full of holes and now it's in a cast
But why are Your gates always higher than us

As we used to talk to each other before
The depth for notions true friendship deepens
Would You tear the tears from my salty fists
The leftovers of my house are just the seeds

If pulling takes longer than pushing
Is it too steep to pull each other to weep
Should I hang on my neck the necklace of hooks
To find someone else—someone else like me

Too many corners all over my house
You drop the sandpaper for my rest
When rubber with leather together are sewn
I need to land on Your ageless nest

When questions question the questions
The docile answer kneels gently on dull knife
When I see You, Lord, my eyes do not blink
For if I blinked I would lose my whole life

Can I still grow up in the same womb
Can I hide inside Your whitest hair
You say the narrow mind passes the answers
And whoever screams cannot see or hear

I see Your hands without the wrinkles, bones, or veins
Just the maps, just events, just the worlds, just the time
I see the waterfalls full of songs under stairs by Your feet
The poems whisper by the millions from Your mouth in rhyme

AKIANE

My child,
Every sweat drop has reached the ditch for flower
Every bridge has held the storm for river
The battles are still won by losing
But the fools still wonder how to maim the sliver

Above the time love wraps infinity
Inside the time love brings the man
Alone with pain everyone gets humbled
Out of the hurricane the rainbow reaches like a hand

Can someone turn away from Me in search of truth
One lie could empty entire eternity
How many shadows will beat against your hearts
When on the ground your tears get dirty

How many springs are in one season
How many eternities can you choose
In the draft even music gets sick
The tables are sturdy because of screws

The minds are losing hearts—the empty wells deceive
The arrows do not show the way to My home
Your fingernails will scratch the scars again
The test will be hard—hold love like a honeycomb

Soon you will become both My silence and My shout
You will live to listen,—you will live to speak My way
Let Me in—Let Me in—You have so much work
My old age will escort you if you obey

———

Spider webs on me—How long did I rest in prayer
Shoes with holes—I have not started walking yet
Inside the saddled journey of the night
Now I can find white blossoms in the net

After that week, there wasn't a single morning in which we missed a fifteen-minute walk to the lake to talk, meditate, and write poetry. The nature and panoramic views profoundly inspired Akiane as she watched eagles trying to separate the bird flocks, or ducklings sunning themselves on the rocks, or trains moving slowly in the distance. Most often she would sit in my lap and admit she was completely empty and had not the slightest new thought in her mind. Then, after a quiet prayer, she would sit still and wait. Maybe half an hour would pass before she squeezed my hand. "I am ready . . . I see so much . . ." And from my pocket I would take a notepad and three pens, just in case one of them would freeze up or leak. Many blizzards, rainstorms, and blistering hot hours were experienced on the pristine shore.

Although she was never inclined to discuss it, Akiane became more and more compelled to write—and I became more and more fascinated with the process. I started noting all of the subtleties involved in her dictation, from the change in intonation of her voice to the variety of her facial expressions. She was never in any hypnotic state—it was obvious that she was not channeling or sleep talking—she was awake and alert, focused and mentally involved. Most of the time her eyes stayed wide open, as if she were watching a big fireworks display or examining something under a microscope. After she finished dictating a poem, she would kiss me on the cheek and we would return home where she would make decisions about the poem's presentation. For example, she might say, "I think this should have five lines in each verse and no capital letters, except for 'God.'"

Another peculiar facet of Akiane's creativity was the matching of her paintings and poetry. Although most poems were not accompanied by paintings, almost every painting was now accompanied by a poem. But how Akiane arrived at her matches mystified everyone. These poems would relate to precise visual or emotional elements of her paintings, but during the writing process she rarely focused on any deliberate parallels. It was as though the conscious matching of poem and painting occurred after both had been completed.

As we watched our daughter grow, we noticed that if she did not paint or write something each day, she felt unfulfilled. These forms of creativity had become a vital outlet for her. While it was somewhat easier to comprehend Akiane's art, which she created for weeks and months at a time, we were never able to understand the source, the method, or the pattern of her writings. As soon as we were convinced that they arrived in a certain way, something would happen to show us that we didn't have the whole

AKIANE

picture. Her prophetic drama zigzagged through what she called "the maze inside the puzzle." Yet as we watched her daily, she appeared to be a typical girl her age and rarely gave the impression of being a serious thinker.

Often Markus and I were both intrigued and disheartened by our daughter's complete indifference to public opinion. One day I noticed that Akiane had referenced the fact that glass was made from sand in her poem "Chipped View." When I asked her how she knew this, she was surprised herself. "I didn't know. Whatever popped into my head, I wrote down. You know that these thoughts just come to me."

"Well, how will you explain what you write to others?" I could just imagine how difficult it would be for others to believe that these poems were actually her work.

"Don't worry. Why do you concern yourself with what other people think? You see, Mama, when you love, you can't describe it either."

Chipped View

If some are chosen to bow down to wear the yokes
Some are chosen to live a spark
The scabs are puzzled everlastingly
Weaned honor is delivered in the midst of dark

Bowing to themselves the crownless kings
Sit in their own bent thrones
As cattle live in castles full of lion clawprints
Life becomes the play with ashes of the drones

Before the glass palaces—the sand
Before ruby swords—the fists
Before the chipped heaven—the chipped view
The nestlings in the marble nests.

Along with her increasing love for writing poetry, Akiane went back to her painting with such drive and stamina that Markus and I had to insist she take breaks from her artistic marathons. "One more shadow—wait, one more minute," she would say, totally engrossed in her own world of forms, colors, and stories. Most often she didn't allow anyone to watch her paint. If we forgot to knock at her door and entered before she had time to turn the easel around, she would be extremely upset. "Out!" she would shout. "Now you've spoiled my surprise. I can't work like this. Everyone is coming and going like weasels by the easels. Leave me alone! Everyone! Please! This is not the post office!"

Disinterested in anyone else's comments or criticism, Akiane worked with confidence far beyond her years. She quickly progressed to larger and larger canvases, painting allegorical scenes, images of nature, and portraits. Meanwhile, she experimented with different media and styles—from expressionistic color sketches to realistic oil paintings.

But despite her dedication, she continued to bewilder us with her complete indifference to the work of other artists. She declined all offers to visit museums or galleries, as well as the chance to study at an art school. Perplexed, we nevertheless arranged for her to take a class from a local artist, but Akiane returned from her first session quivering with indignation. "It was the dumbest lesson in my life. The teacher held on to my hand the whole time. That isn't teaching—that's cheating! I don't need teachers. I need students." She looked again at the watercolor landscape she had done in the class and tore it in two.

The same week over a dozen neighborhood children came for her art classes.

The Prince of Peace

One of the most uncanny events surrounding Akiane's art was her discovery of one particular model. Desperately wanting to paint portraits of Jesus, whom she had first seen in her dreams, she spent a lot of time searching for the right face. For over a year she had been looking for the perfect representation of Jesus; she stood by supermarkets, shopping malls, parks, and on city streets, watching thousands of faces pass by, only to shake her head.

One morning she asked us to pray with her throughout the day about her Jesus model. "I can't do this anymore, God. This is it. I can't find anyone by myself," eight-and-a-half-year-old Akiane tearfully prayed. "I need You to send me the right model and give me the right idea. Maybe it's too much to ask, but could You send him right through our front door? Yes, right through our front door."

AKIANE

The very next day, in the middle of the afternoon, the doorbell rang and an acquaintance brought her friend, a carpenter, right through our front door. She introduced him to Akiane, thinking that the young artist would like his features. Standing almost seven feet tall, the carpenter had strong hands and a warm smile.

"*Tai jis!* This is he!" Akiane blushed.

"*Kas jis?* Who is he?" I asked her quietly in Lithuanian.

"*Tai vyras kuris modeliuos Jezaus paveikslui. Labai panasus i mano pasikartojancias vizijas.* This is the man who'll model for the Jesus painting. He resembles the image that keeps coming back to me in my visions. Maybe he's the reason God moved us to this town."

We were stunned at the prompt response to our prayers. In our excitement, we all touched the man to make sure he was real and that we were not dreaming. He was in jeans, a white T-shirt, and a pair of old sneakers. His voice was deep and peaceful, and though he said only a few words, we learned that his life was quite extraordinary. Yet what struck us most was his demeanor—a balance of meekness and poise.

After he left, Akiane couldn't find words to describe her thankfulness. She stayed in her bedroom for hours, sketching all possible angles for her future portrait. But a week later the carpenter called her to apologize, stating that he felt unworthy to represent his Master, and that he had to decline the honor. We were all disappointed, but Akiane refused to give up, praying even more feverishly that day, the next day, and the next.

Another week passed before the carpenter called us back. "God wants me to do it, but I have only three days before I have to cut my hair and beard."

Akiane couldn't have been happier. Soon afterward, she choreographed the poses, studied the carpenter's face, and took several pictures. She was anxious to begin her sketching and right away decided to start with the resurrection scene for the *Prince of Peace* painting.

We were amazed by the quick pace at which she was working. She was so pleased about her progress that she even allowed us to videotape her. It took her only forty hours to finish the portrait, but in that short period of time she lost a total of four baby teeth— a tooth for each ten hours of painting. At one point, desperately needing a thin brush to paint eyelashes, she even cut a strand of her own hair and made a fine brush. Watching the portrait develop was almost like watching a microscopic embryo develop into a newborn. Physically, artistically, and logically, the process of her painting was incomprehensible, as though the Almighty power was vibrating through her every vein.

AKIANE

While the painting was drying on the white wall of the studio, every viewer was quick to notice that no matter where you stood, Jesus's eyes followed you. Although the portrait resembled the model, Akiane had altered his expression and features to mimic the resurrected Jesus she remembered from her dream. Many times we overheard Akiane share the meaning to others. "The light side of His face represents heaven. And the dark side represents suffering on earth. His light eye in the dark shows that He's with us in all our troubles, and He is the Light when we need Him."

Upon completion of this painting, Akiane immediately began sketching the profile for her next portrait of Jesus. The position of the hands in the composition turned out to be an enormous challenge for her. Our bedroom was adjacent to Akiane's studio, so very early in the morning we would hear *bam, bam, bam* into the wall. We knew this sound well; she was blending on the canvas. But no matter how difficult an area of the painting was for her, she never gave up and kept repeating, "I want this portrait to look real. Real, real, real, real! . . . He has to lift up the world to His Father with strong hands. Strong hands!"

At one point, while she struggled to represent the hands, Akiane decided to add more red but had run out of paint and walnut oil. I quickly ran to the store to get the correct shade she'd requested, but when I returned home, I discovered I'd bought the wrong hue. A frustrated Akiane sent me back to the store, but what I brought home was once again the wrong color. What made it so difficult was that Akiane didn't even know the names of most of her paints. To give me a guide for my next trip to the art store, she went to the kitchen, took a steak knife, nipped her thumb a bit, and squeezed out a droplet of blood onto my hand. "This is the exact color I need—and hurry, before the color changes!"

Akiane working on her second painting of Jesus, titled Father Forgive Them

When the body was almost finished, she spent the whole week experimenting with the background. After adding, removing, and again adding a beam of light from His eyes, she decided to remove it. "We can't see that. It's only Jesus who sees that light. Let people imagine what's behind the black." So she mixed some blue with black and, from her ladder, painted over the beam for the last time.

Our family still couldn't afford a professional easel, so Akiane was working on the easel her dad had built from scrap wood. It was very difficult for us to hold ourselves back

AKIANE

from complaining about the mess that was spreading throughout the whole ranch. The chairs, tables, bedcovers, dishes, towels, and doorknobs all tracked Akiane's whereabouts with smears of oil paint. But we all knew how exhausted she was after painting, so her brothers graciously began taking turns washing the oily brushes and glass palettes.

Many people began coming to see Akiane. All of them said the same thing: "We can watch this process, but we still don't believe it. It's impossible. We wonder how others, who *haven't* seen how she works, could ever believe it."

We shipped the *Prince of Peace* to an art agent who had agreed to represent Akiane's work and who had promised to find a buyer for the painting. But when he found out that Akiane had begun painting yet another Jesus portrait, he became angry. We felt strongly that we needed to find another agent. When we asked him to release us, he refused. "I will not terminate the contract," he roared. "According to the agreement, she'll have to wait nine more years . . . unless you want to buy me out for $100,000?" Then he threatened to keep *The Prince of Peace* as long as he cared to, asserting his authority as the manager. Unexpectedly, Jesus had become a hostage.

After praying for the safe return of the painting, a chain reaction of the most unusual events led to the arrival of the semi-dried oil of Jesus on our front doorstep— exactly on the day of Akiane's birthday. The painting was delivered in a bent crate full of sawdust, so a tearful but relieved Akiane had to work hours with a vacuum cleaner and dry brush to clean it up. "My goodness! He looks just like after the Crucifixion . . . full of sawdust . . . We are going to *resurrect* Him. No . . . He is going to resurrect Himself. Hmm . . . It took me forty hours to paint this painting and seventy hours to paint *Father Forgive Them*. The numbers mean something, but I can't remember what . . ." Akiane squinted. Miraculously she was able to lift all of the embedded sawdust from the surface, and soon she was able to celebrate her ninth birthday, not with candles, but with two Jesus paintings.

Many months later, thousands of people were discussing the two portraits of Jesus. Among them were scientists from Russia who noted that Akiane's *Prince of Peace* had a remarkable resemblance to the mysterious image taken from the very Shroud of Turin. Puzzled scholars from India were fascinated by Akiane's depiction of a towel robe, for, according to them—and unknown to Akiane—adult Jews wore similar robes during worship two thousand years ago. In addition, hundreds of people from all over the world wrote to Akiane saying they were shown this exact portrait during their dreams.

AKIANE

The Stage

Soon we looked for a miracle to find a way to break away from the art agent. We had no resources, for Markus had recently been injured at his job and was at home with us. Another child prodigy "expert" suddenly appeared in our lives, but he was mostly interested in the expressionistic paintings that Akiane sometimes created at one sitting between her more time-consuming works. Since Akiane did not want anyone to see these rapid color sketches, which she often called "immature," she preferred to hide them in her closet or under her desk. Nevertheless, before long the new agent agreed to represent Akiane and offered to help obtain an expensive legal separation from the previous manager. Rationalizing and pushing aside the red flags, we decided to try out the new agent.

At this same time, an unexpected thing happened. Our family had sent news about Akiane to the media, and in response, nine-year-old Akiane was invited to appear on *The Oprah Winfrey Show* in a segment called "The Most Talented Kids in the World."

On the day of the shoot, Akiane stepped out of a black limousine onto the Chicago streets and into the studio, with her huge paintings arriving separately in seven-foot crates. The media staff placed a wireless microphone transmitter under Akiane's navy blue dress, and the makeup artist combed her straight hair. "You're too beautiful for makeup," she said, smearing some Vaseline on Akiane's lips. In the Green Room one of the youngest and most famous fashion designers in the world kissed Akiane's hands. "Oh, my goodness! So these are the hands that created the most astonishing paintings in history! You are a true genius!"

I pulled Akiane aside. "Remember," I whispered, "your new agent told us that you shouldn't focus on God so that you don't offend the viewers of different beliefs. Remember when I used to be very offended myself by just hearing the word *God*? Do you know who Oprah is?"

"No, yes, no!" Akiane was in a whirlwind.

"You'll like her." I stopped there; I didn't want Akiane to realize right then and there that this was one of the most popular and beloved television shows in the world—a show on which many professionals dream of appearing. I didn't want to start explaining how legendary this courageous woman was until the lights and cameras were off.

Before we knew it, Akiane was climbing onto the stage in her new velvet dress. At the end of the interview, Oprah asked, "Where does your inspiration come from?"

AKIANE

"From God." Akiane couldn't keep from mentioning the most important influence in her life.

"From God . . . ," Oprah repeated and hugged her.

We flew home from Chicago enlivened but exhausted, only to find that the ABC television crew would be coming over in a few days to videotape Akiane. Shortly after this, CNN's crew came and filmed Akiane for an entire day in preparation for the feature story of the *Lou Dobbs Show*. When Akiane was painting *The Journey,* the producers were immensely interested in watching her painting process. After hours and hours of videotaping her painting and talking, the producers admitted that they'd never seen a child who could endure such a long day of interviews.

Following this, Akiane was invited to many other shows. After one of them, on the plane back home, she saw the city from above and asked, "Mom, where do people go to pray? It's all concrete for miles. Where's the pen? Could you write down a few sentences for me?"

Akiane put her head on my lap and closed her eyes. She had developed a high fever, but she just had to get the poem out. My head was spinning as well, but I pulled out a blunt pencil from my pocket. Akiane dictated in Lithuanian, because she didn't want others around us to understand what she was saying. Within a few minutes, *The Stage* was effortlessly dictated to me. Then she stopped and looked at me with her red and runny eyes. "*Am I too young to be found?* Put that down. That's the end!" And Akiane fell fast asleep.

The Stage

The howling eyes forecast the plainest heart
And I forget my chivalry monsoon.
Crippled meaning of my brittle bravery
Shrinks cowardly with every balding noon.

I creep under lost victory
To hear bitter beats of drumming theft.
Throughout my courage traffic changes lanes
If I forget which role I left.

The mass of the self never ends . . .
Shall I put on the mask to complete the face?
All of a sudden on a stage of words
The meaning becomes just a dress in lace . . .

Lusterless gazes beat like weakened wings
Against the pillow curtains of a pulpit dump.
The rhythm of the chaos lacerates aroma
Till it becomes a fragrance stump . . .

The fresh cut could still be smelled—
But the profile of the sound hides like a fraud.
In front of lenses—the close-up of the rouge
The flatter still pretending to applaud

The drama map reveals how long I will spin
On a blank canvas of the stage like dice.
As I drill the brush into the sketch, I drizzle
And my dew veil covers the coconut eyes . . .

I bolt my fingers into the lame horizon of the audience
Where ovation changes like an illusionist's hand
I mime around until I smell the tangled hair
All pulled into the theater fan.

Am I landing on a stepping pedestal of mystery
Where truth with frosted hair dives blue face down?
The wrinkles show up with each flicker of the candle—
If I left them for God—am I too young to be found?

Jesus's Missing Years

Within a few short months the second art manager stopped representing our daughter, and we were on our own again. As Markus worked full-time at the hospital

AKIANE

and I homeschooled, we continued to help Akiane with her art shows. Before her tenth birthday Akiane embarked on another painting of Jesus—this time showing Him as a very young man during His missing years. A few weeks after she had started the painting, something about it began to upset her. The near-finished portrait was losing its charm, and Akiane was ready to gesso over the whole canvas and start over. "Who knows why this is happening? Maybe I'm experiencing the hardship that a teenage Jesus had to go through. I think I'm feeling His anguish." The entire month was filled with artistic frustration, but at the end of it Akiane worked out the problem areas and began aggressively repairing the whole face and figure, brushstroke by brushstroke.

As I was sweeping one afternoon, I overheard Akiane talking with her three-year-old brother, Ilia. "Why am I laboring over this painting? I'll just paint two ears and call it *The Missing Ears*. It'll be so easy."

"Isn't today your day off?" I asked.

"Yes, today I play."

"Are you playing right now?"

"I am. Today I'll play on the canvas. Didn't Jesus make exceptions on Sabbath when He healed people? I am painting Him, after all. And maybe this painting will even heal someone." She wiped the excess paint from her brush, not on a paper towel, but right on the canvas itself, leaving streaks of different colors by the figure. Then she quickly ran outside and brought a few children into her studio to ask their opinion about Jesus's age, and everyone agreed that He looked many years older if you stood at a distance from the painting. But Akiane corrected them. "He is timeless—and because of that, you can catch a glimpse of Him as a teenager and an adult all at once."

With one big mirror at the end of her studio and a smaller one in her right hand, she was meticulously checking the slightest inaccuracies. "I have to blend the sides of the lower lips with the skin a little more," she explained, scratching her paint-splattered forehead, "and then it should look more natural."

"I've noticed that you are getting more patient. By the time you finish this work, it could reach . . ."

"Two-hundred hours! That's what, three months now?" Akiane completed the sentence. "You know, I decided not to rush. The turtle wins the race, right?"

"Usually, yes, if its shell isn't too heavy."

"This isn't abstract art. This is realism: it takes time."

Later that day when I was kissing Akiane good night, I began asking her about one planet on her canvas.

"Oh, that's the new earth. I just felt that I had to include it. I don't remember where, when, or how, but the earth will change. All I know is that everything will be different. There will be no fear, no hatred, and no hunger or pain. Only love."

"Why is it all green? I see no blue oceans."

"I don't know. Maybe only rivers and lakes will be there. Why do you ask me as if I know? I paint what I can remember from my visions."

"Is your Jesus looking at the galaxies?"

Akiane closed her eyes. "No, that's behind Him."

"Then what is He looking at?"

"I'll tell you tomorrow."

I gently pulled open one eyelid to get her attention. "What is He looking at?"

"Mom, you have no imagination . . ."

"You aren't asleep yet. Go ahead, tell me."

"I'm sleeping."

"No, you're not."

"Tomorrow!"

"Please!"

"You have no patience, Mama. He is talking with His Father in heaven. Haven't you seen His footsteps from the earth to where He is talking with His Father about the future of our world? I think Jesus will come back in full power very soon. In the back of Him you can see the whole birth process of our new universe."

"Why is the new earth behind some clouds?"

"It's hidden for now." She pulled her blanket off her bed and, with a down pillow held between her teeth, tiptoed to our bedroom to lie down.

God, Why Akiane?

Although Akiane was sure about her unique abilities, there were many days when she questioned her mission. One morning as we were wiping up a spill by her easel, Akiane wondered aloud, "Why was I chosen instead of some other child?"

AKIANE

"Akiane, I have no clue. The more I know, the less I understand. You hated traveling; now you travel. You were shy, and now you're on the stage surrounded by people and cameras. You were stubborn about chores, and now you paint for months to create detailed pictures. Your weakness was language, and now you not only create poetry but spend hours talking to people about deeply profound issues. You had a hard time remembering, and now you've learned sign language on your own. You were strong-willed, and now you hear and obey God. Why was weak David chosen to fight giant Goliath?"

"I still feel like I'm the wrong person. Someone else would be much better." As we scrubbed the floor, she spoke in English. Lately she preferred using her dad's native tongue.

"Maybe God looks at your heart." I kissed her.

The next day was very cold and rainy. My sons came to pray with me by the harvested and plowed farm field approximately a half-mile away from our house. It was usual for us to spend every morning with nature no matter what the weather was like. This day Akiane didn't show up. An hour later, totally drenched with rain, I came home and saw my daughter signing on the left bottom corner of the canvas. Usually that meant she was going to finish the painting within a few days. I tried to ignore the mess surrounding her, but then I heard *splash!* Right before my eyes she dropped a paper-plate palette full of paint on the floor, and now it was lying upside down. I picked up two dried-up filbert paintbrushes and an unscrewed paint tube by the recliner and looked at her impatiently.

"Please, leave me by myself!" she said, raising her high-pitched voice. Similar reactions were usual, but I had learned long ago that arguing with her at such times was pointless. No reprimands, corrections, punishments, or consequences had ever affected her. She had absolutely no fear. She paid serious attention only to gentleness, prayer, and love. A simple hug with a kiss was always more powerful than any reprimand, grounding, chore, or loss of favorite activities. Sometimes it looked to us as if her heavenly Father Himself was the one bringing her up—as if He, not we, was her main authority. She always lived in a world quite different from the one we provided for her.

We had never seen a child so stubborn yet so lighthearted, so strong-willed yet so loving, so witty yet so childish, so independent yet so social, so introverted and yet so friendly. "God, why her?" we often asked Him, bewildered by her complex character.

Later that night, as I was kissing Akiane good night, I mentioned to her that the Crystal Cathedral had invited her to visit.

AKIANE

"How many people will see me?"

"About four thousand in the audience and about ten million on TV."

"Sometimes I just wish I could be a normal kid, and no one would see me and no one would talk about me. Yet I feel God wants me to do it."

I hugged her and told her that many inspired Muslims, Buddhists, and atheists had written thank-you letters to her. But Akiane was not surprised—she explained to me that it had to be this way. As she curled up into a ball, I kissed her on her forehead. I was suddenly taken by the feeling that I didn't want her to grow up.

"Can I sleep with you and Ilia tonight?" she asked.

"I would be delighted, if you don't mind your brother giving you another black eye while he sleep-fights."

"Do you know what my brothers are saving their money for?"

"For land?"

"No, for my paintings and prints so they too can send money to poor kids." She lay down and fell asleep almost instantly. The rock necklace she'd recently polished for herself was still strung around her neck. Her hair was uncombed, and her blouse was splattered with fresh paint. As she lay on her back, she breathed quietly next to her snoring baby brother. I felt I could understand her better when she slept. Then I was able to hold her hand and talk to her, and she couldn't hear me.

"I Belong to God"

By now Akiane was ten years old, and word about her had begun to spread to museums. Before long she was invited to the Museum of Religious Art in Iowa, and the three-day exhibition proved to be an unforgettable event.

The minute we reached the museum, we saw a full parking lot and masses of people standing in a line that wound from the outside doors down the road—and the line was getting longer with every passing minute. Thousands of people stood for many hours just to get Akiane's autograph. Visitors had arrived from various states, and some had flown in from the West and East Coasts. There were doctors and artists, mayors and professors, art collectors and lawyers, journalists and executives, students and toddlers. There were handicapped people in wheelchairs; there were elderly folks with their walk-

AKIANE

ers—even a 102-year-old grandmother. Several teenagers attended the exhibition, drawing in their sketchbooks as they observed her images displayed on the high walls.

Men and women alike were deeply moved as they passed by our daughter and her huge paintings. Everybody wanted to ask her questions. One crippled lady stood up from her wheelchair for the first time in many years just to have her picture taken next to Akiane. There were also numerous people who asked the young artist to bless or heal their families and to pray for their problems and illnesses. The museum staff paced around astonished at the number of people who had shown up at the event.

The questions poured in to Akiane from all directions. "What church do you belong to? What denomination?" someone from the crowd asked loudly.

"I belong to God," Akiane responded.

"Do you relate better to adults or to your peers?"

"To adults and to babies."

"What do you think about the future of the United States and the rest of the world?" another person asked.

"I forget all my visions, but I believe there are some answers in my art and poetry."

Akiane and a 102-year-old grandmother at the Museum of Religious Art exhibition

"I am a Buddhist. You called Jesus the "Prince of Peace," yet in His name so many people were massacred. How do you explain that?"

"Jesus is peace, just like calm water. But anyone can drop a stone into water and make it muddy."

"Why did you choose Christianity instead of another religion?"

"I didn't choose Christianity; I chose Jesus Christ. I am painting and writing what God shows me. I don't know much about the religions, but I know this: God looks at our love."

"Have you seen UFOs, since I see you've painted a few right here?"

"I don't know what they are, and I don't remember if I've painted them. If I did, that means there is a reason, but people have to solve that reason by themselves. Each inch I paint on my canvas—whether it's about pain, joy, or mystery—is meaningful and is directed by God."

"How would you describe your style of painting?" came another question.

"Akianism—a blend of realism and imagination."

"What do you like painting most?"

"Faces. They are more meaningful to me than anything else. A face is the first thing you see when you are born. We cannot live fully without seeing or touching a human face."

"Who taught you how to paint?"

"I'm self-taught. In other words, God is my teacher."

"What message do you want people to get from your art and poetry?"

"I want my art to draw people's attention to God, and I want my poetry to keep their attention on God."

Amazingly, the constant attention, handshaking, and autographing did not wear Akiane down. After three days of commotion, which included an auction, a television show appearance, and interviews for *Time* magazine and other publications, we flew home in a daze. Back at home we went through the many gifts Akiane had received throughout the trip. One gift bag in particular moved us; it contained a photo of a ten-year-old boy who had brought his family to the museum. He was curious to see a girl his age who could paint better than he could—he was so captivated that he even insisted on coming the second day as well. We could remember him admiring Akiane's paintings and speaking to her on several occasions. Then moments after he left the museum, due to a previously undetected malignant brain stem tumor, he had a stroke and was immediately rushed to the hospital. During this time, the boy was greatly comforted by the memories from the museum exhibition and Akiane's love for God. Before he died, the final thing he wanted to do was to draw.

Doors to Faith

With the increasing international media exposure and many solo art shows across the country, our family's life has become more and more public. Ten-year-old Akiane's works have been displayed in galleries, museums, auctions, and private collections around the world, with prices for her art reaching into six figures. She was inducted into The Kids Hall of Fame, has published her first book, the one you now hold in your hands, and is regarded as the youngest binary prodigy in both realistic art and poetry in recorded history.

Yet surprisingly it is not our zealous efforts, but rather our patience and continuous prayers that have been rewarded. Whenever we tried to move Akiane's mission forward to help God, the doors were consistently closed. But whenever we stopped pushing them, God opened them up and blessed us. The best opportunities always came through His timing and direction—not ours.

As Akiane's parents, we watch with wonder as Akiane continues to develop and mature. Before the public recognition, Akiane's life was quite simple. Now, with various documentaries and the media coverage—interviews, appearances, traveling, autograph signing, and charity events, all that has changed. There are prints to proof and sign; paintings to create; art exhibitions, schools, and universities to attend; and thousands of e-mails and letters to answer from fans, academies, hospitals, prisons, churches, government agencies, and entertainment studios. Yet Akiane herself somehow seems to remain completely unaffected by all the public attention and recognition. She sees it all as just "another skip over the rope."

For some reason, ordinary people have been able to understand Akiane's deep and complex poetry. We notice that the message of faith is recognized by people of all religious and philosophical viewpoints, and the art is absorbed easily by both young and old. We watch in awe as again and again our child tells people that her gifts come from God, and that if she has been blessed, there is one reason and one reason only: to help others.

Although most of her work is serious, people meeting Akiane find her totally carefree, humble, vivacious, and lighthearted. They don't see a philosopher or an eccentric artist, but rather a playful young girl who enjoys many different things, such as playing chess, composing on the piano, weaving, cooking, or just dreaming. It seems that all along, God's protection of Akiane's childhood innocence has been through her selective memory—something that had so worried us for many years. For how else could a child show awareness of such intense adult emotions and spiritual events without any negative consequences afterward? It's another mystery, yet anyone who knows Akiane observes how easygoing and unself-conscious she is, how she loves people, and how young children knock on her door every day just to play with her or watch her entertain them, covered from head to toe with paint, like a living canvas.

For the first eight years we were frustrated with the peculiar circumstances that led to Akiane's lack of exposure to other children her age, but now we see God's wisdom in closing those doors. How else would we have been convinced that both her spiritual and artistic transformation came directly from our Father in heaven and not from our own neighborhood or society? We believe our daughter's work is significant because of the absolute impossibility that she could create as she does without divine inspiration. Almost every person we meet asks if we as parents are proud of Akiane, and almost every time we find it difficult to answer this simple question. We feel blessed to participate in our daughter's mission, but we don't feel proud, as none of this has come from our own efforts.

Akiane continues to believe that without dreams there is no hope and there is no tomorrow, that dreams are the doors to faith. She believes she is led to help other families get closer to the Creator. She believes everyone has some talent they can cultivate and use to serve others.

Akiane is convinced that the greatest gift we could give to God, who has everything and does not need anything except our love, is for us to love one another and walk in faith, day by day, hour by hour. Now we, as her parents, believe that too. For by trusting Akiane and by listening to her messages, which were divinely inspired yet masked with childish laughter, we were rewarded with one of the greatest gifts of all: faith.

The Kramarik family

AKIANE

akiane
her art

The Hollow Compasses · AGE 6

(oil pastel on paper; 14" x 20")

The Empathy · AGE 6

(oil pastel on paper; 12" x 18")

The Life · AGE 6

(oil pastel on paper; 9.5" x 12")

The Rainbow River
AGE 6
(oil pastel on paper; 30" x 36")

The Growth (self-portrait)
AGE 6
(oil pastel on paper; 30" x 36")

AKIANE

The Waiting • AGE 6

(oil pastel on paper; 30" x 36")

The Raking • AGE 6

(oil pastel on paper; 30" x 36")

AKIANE

Again I Find the Winter · AGE 7

(acrylic on canvas; 18" x 24")

When I was seven, we had one accident and illness after another in our family—and once we even got lost in the Colorado Mountains. I was so car sick from all the switchbacks, but then I saw a lake through the trees. When we finally found our way back home, I knew what my first acrylic painting would be. I thought that with this poem and painting I would speak about love while we must wait in pain and suffering.

The Footsteps of Spring · AGE 7

(acrylic on canvas; 20" x 30")

AKIANE

The Dreamfence · AGE 7
(acrylic on canvas; 26" x 36")

When I was seven, a neighbor gave us a strawberry-red kitten. We called him Charlie. He was the best cat anyone could have— smart, cuddly, and cute. But after a month, due to my father's and my baby brother's severe allergies, we had to find another home for our kitty. I was very sad, so I wrote a good-bye letter to him, saying that I hoped he would find a good family. Soon I painted two kittens so both Charlie and I would feel better. Dreams do come true; a little later I saw Charlie playing with a white kitten with tiger stripes on a neighbor's porch.

The Horse · AGE 7
(acrylic on board; 22" x 34")

One day on a farm, I saw one horse. I don't know why it appeared funny to me at that time.

AKIANE

The Eagle · AGE 7

(acrylic on board; 9" x 12")

Each · AGE 7

(acrylic on canvas; 18" x 24")

My father was injured and without a job, my baby brother was very sick, my mom was homeschooling us four children, and we were very poor. I was seven and stubborn. I wanted to paint, but we had no money for paints or canvases. I found in the garage a small canvas and two semi-empty pails of paint—one white, the other burnt umber. I painted this landscape to show how each day is important, whether we are rich or poor, sad or happy, because we grow from all our experiences. Right after finishing this painting, I decided to teach small children art to raise money for my art supplies.

AKIANE

Strength · AGE 7 (acrylic on canvas; 30" x 40")

The wild cats are so mysterious. I wanted to show the strength of a lion that I envisioned in the new earth. No longer does he need to kill so that he can feed his family. He needs to be who he is: gentle and strong with love in his eyes. I painted the reflection of his cubs in his bright irises to show that he must be strong for them.

Akiane

Color Sketches, and Expressionistic paintings

The paintings on this page are studies of various subjects created in one sitting.

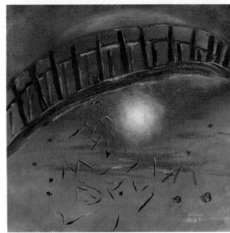

AKIANE

The Clematis Dream · AGE 8 (Oil on canvas; 36" x 48")

In the Japanese garden in our backyard, I noticed one clematis flower that seemed to be floating in the air. The next morning I woke up from a strange dream, wrote it down with a chalk on the window, and began painting the blossom. Much later I realized that the clematis flower in my dream represented love and trust.

AKIANE

Listening · AGE 8 (acrylic on canvas; 36" x 48")

I was hoping to create an allegory about listening with this majestic tiger. The orange is the color of listening, the black stripes are the lies, and the white represents the truth. Listening to the lies and the truth as the stripes and the fur intertwine is difficult. But not for someone who is peaceful, wise, and attentive like tiger. This portrait represents the noble leaders, kings, and emperors who listen to the needs of their "jungle."

AKIANE

Life Without a Leash · AGE 8 (acrylic on canvas; 36" x 48")

From the time we first got our golden retriever, Simba, he's always been so loyal and brave. And with those begging eyes, he knows very well how to get from me anything he wants. One day when I picked out the four-foot-long canvas at the art supply store, I knew I wanted to paint him twice his real size. And that's how he seemed to me every day: noble and big-hearted. It was my first huge painting and one of the easiest to paint. When he saw himself, he licked the corner of the canvas, as if to show me where I should sign—and that's when I decided the painting was finished.

AKIANE

The Planted Eyes
AGE 8
(Oil on canvas; 36" x 48")

In THE PLANTED EYES I wanted to express the beauty and the suffering of the black race. It was my fastest portrait—it took me only fifteen hours from the sketch to the very end. It was also my first oil painting and Oprah's favorite. You can see the whole life of this African woman in her eyes, which are full of strength and spirituality. The red outfit portrays her love, the gold earring portrays her inner richness and confidence, the deep wrinkle in the forehead portrays the deep tragedy in her life, the gray hair portrays her wisdom, and the background stripes portray the hardships.

My Sight Cannot Wait for Me
AGE 8
(acrylic on canvas; 36" x 48")

I wanted to paint myself, first of all, because I was the only one available to model at that time, and I also wanted people to get to know me better. My self-portrait shows my relationship with God.

AKIANE

Akiane at work on Father Forgive Them.

Akiane painting her self-portrait.

AKIANE

Progression of *Prince of Peace*

Prince of Peace: The Resurrection • AGE 8 (oil on canvas; 36" x 48")

AKIANE

Father Forgive Them • AGE 9 (oil on canvas; 48" x 60")

AKIANE

The Summer Snow
AGE 9
(acrylic on canvas; 26" x 46")

The story of a hummingbird rescuing a flower from a summer snow was created in a few days after a hail like snow crushed all our flowers in the garden. As one hummingbird was still circling around the most beautiful blossom, I immediately ran to my studio and grabbed my brush to play with my paints.

AKIANE

Faith • AGE 9 (oil on canvas; 54" x 54")

Tied up to a board and thrown out to die on the dirt road, this baby girl was crying for days somewhere in Asia before she was found. When I met her many months later, I knew at once that I would paint her in an empty field, away from the big city, where she'd find God and love for the first time. I dedicate this painting to all the abandoned babies and children—it is because of our selfishness that they suffer and die.

AKIANE

The Evening Swan • AGE 9 (acrylic on canvas; 54" x 54")

One evening a swan flew by me so closely that I was able to feel her feathers. I felt quite lonely that night, feeling a huge difference between what I saw in heaven and what I saw on earth. She was the answer to my prayers.

AKIANE

The Dance of the Mind Inside the White · AGE 9 (oil on canvas; 25" x 25")

It seemed as if I painted these flowers in one breath and in one brushstroke. The oils were flowing and blending so fast that it appeared as if the image itself spoke, "Don't touch me anymore. Enough."

AKIANE

Bald • AGE 9   (acrylic on canvas; 25" x 25")

In one of my visions I saw an eagle flying through a huge city full of skyscrapers and sharing his secrets of the future, but by the time I started painting the image, I could no longer remember his words.

AKIANE

The Freedom Horse · AGE 9 (acrylic on canvas; 30" x 40")

When for the first time in my life I was invited to ride a horse on a farm, I felt such freedom! But then it occurred to me that the horse would feel free only without me on his back—somewhere in the wild. It reminded me about love: to truly love we have to be free . . . to truly appreciate love we have to be free when we choose right from wrong. We can be forced to obey, but we cannot be forced to love.

AKIANE

The Antlers • AGE 9 (acrylic on canvas; 48" x 60")

This is another allegory about friendship and love, about family and its hardships, and about the races and their interactions. I mixed up both the white-tailed deer and the mule deer to show the friendship between the races and peace between the countries. The twenty-four deer represent the time—the earthly cycle of twenty-four hours in each day. The green color represents peace. The sunshine on the grass and leaves represents energy and joy. The three paths represent the Trinity. And I painted the entire cycle of a deer's life: the rut, the birth, and the life of a deer from one year to very old age. Only one young buck has noticed that some-one is observing their herd. The deer in his prime in front is telling the story of his life.

AKIANE

The Light-Bearers · AGE 9 (oil on canvas; 48" x 48")

This painting is an allegory about five groups of human beings responding differently to God. When the light representing God shines from above, only three groups notice it. One group runs away from it, even risking life. The next gets very angry as it roars, and the third has their heads raised in awe, wonder, and joy. The mother and her cub are the only ones with the shadow. The other two groups haven't noticed the light at all. They are the fighters, busy fighting to get things, and the selfish ones are just taking care of themselves. So the moral of this painting is this: Don't run away from the light, don't be angry at the light, don't fight or think of only yourself—otherwise you'll miss the light completely. Look up to truth to live, and you will find peace and joy. (When by accident I cut my finger, I decided to sign a second signature with my blood on the trout.)

AKIANE

Courage · AGE 9 (acrylic on canvas; 30" x 40")

To me swans are always full of strength, grace, beauty, love, and courage. In my painting they represent people in the flight of love—the flight between people and races, the islands and the continents, the planets and galaxies is only for the brave. Maybe that's how bridges are built—crossing by faith first.

AKIANE

Silence · AGE 9 (acrylic on canvas; 30" x 40")

There is probably no such place as I painted here, but I wanted to show a scene that I'd envisioned in my mind for a long time. It's more expressionistic than realistic, and that's the way I wanted it to be left—a place where empty silence could also be mistaken, a place where through the sounds of nature you could hear a different silence, a heavenly and living silence.

AKIANE

The Journey · AGE 9 (acrylic on canvas; 48" x 60")

As I was diving underwater one day, I met the most beautiful child. He will be in space, *I thought.* I will paint him, and through him I will share my own story and vision. *I later found out that I'd called the painting* Journey *for a reason. This was because the painting one day became lost, and after quite a while it was found miraculously on the other side of the world.*

AKIANE

Found • AGE 9

(acrylic on canvas; 48" x 60")

I was inspired to paint all the races, but finding black people where I lived in Idaho was very difficult. After a lot of prayers, I finally met two African children whose story was so amazing that I wanted to paint it right away. There was a taboo in their small Madagascar tribe against saving orphans, so after their parents died, the two-year-old brother had to take care of his three-month-old sister for more than two months. When they were found, they were barely alive. I painted them older and healthier to create what their vision might have been during the three-month survival. The baby girl has noticed the help approaching and is gently caressing her exhausted brother to lift his head up. After I invited the adoptive parents to look at the finished portrait, they cried. Although I had painted and gessoed over five different backgrounds for the painting, including deserts, animals, birds, and prairies, I finally decided to paint the waterfalls. Everybody—including me—was surprised at the painted waterfalls in the background, because I had not known that the orphans had been found in the only waterfall jungle in Madagascar.

AKIANE

JeShUa— ThE . . . mIsSiNg . . . YeArS . . . • AGE 10 (acrylic on canvas; 48" x 60")

In a vision I saw Jesus at 14, during one of his meditations, talking with His Father in heaven about the new earth, where only joy and peace will reign. In the background, the galactic hand is reaching out for love and truth.

AKIANE

The Creation · AGE 10 (acrylic on canvas; 48" x 48")

At the beginning of my painting, I was sure only that I would paint space, but I had no ideas or expectations for how the finished story and details would look. After three weeks, I disguised my signature around some planets and even hid a miniature astronaut for those who like to walk with the magnifying glass by my paintings looking for my second signature. Upon completing the painting, I was quite surprised that I had painted the very creation of the universe.

AKIANE

The Connection · AGE 10 (acrylic on canvas; 36" x 48")

In one of my visions, the word connection was flashing in the colors and details of one allegory that I immediately transformed onto canvas. The communion, the attention, and the action formed a connection between three birds. One of the birds was calling and communing, the second one was focusing and giving all her attention, and the third was acting and flying to help. The planets in the sky were also forming a ripple effect of the same connection. But without the communion, the attention, and the action, we cannot have a true connection.

AKIANE

The Angel · AGE 10 (acrylic on canvas; 48" x 48")

Sometimes we meet certain angels that appear as humans and we don't realize it. Many of us have been saved from accidents and we don't know it either. We should appreciate each safe moment. In this painting I blended a few dimensions to portray the guardian angels' mission; with wings invisible to human eyes, yet with the see-through energy veil, the youthful angel is catching a falling child without any tension, difficulty, or worry. That's why I painted her hands in a relaxed manner. The background is gold, copper, and brass. And they signify the providence, the law, and the safety. Saving our bodies is easy for an angel, but what is hard is that sometimes she must allow someone to fall or get hurt, according to God's laws.

AKIANE

The Power of Prayer · AGE 10 (acrylic on canvas; 36" x 48")

The birds in this painting represent prayers. The power of prayer is direction, humility, sincerity, and faith. These birds, just like prayers seeking God, are flying toward the light. Some birds are focused on their destinations, some are distracted, others are playfully soaring, and still others are disappointed and turning back. Once in flight the birds will have to listen to God's quiet voice to know where to find Him. If they are anxious and angry, they will crash against the steep mountains. If they lack faith, they will drown in the river. If they fly just for fun or vain curiosity, they will not hear the spiritual warnings and fly into each other. If they fly just to show off, they will be the first to burn up by God's most intense energy. Unless they are humble and trusting, they will not be accepted by the Light. The force of the fastest and most dedicated prayers is melting the snow off the mountains and cliffs. The more prayers, the more power. The snow in this particular painting represents confusion, hardship, and unhappiness. Half of the ridges are almost free of snow, and as the birds come closer to the light, all of the landscape is becoming full of summer waterfalls and flowers.

AKIANE

The Hourglass · AGE 10 (acrylic on canvas; 36" x 48")

The underwater light formed in the shape of the hourglass represents eternity. The bottom of the hourglass, by the rocks and open shells, represents the past eternity. While the top of the hourglass, close to the surface, represents the future eternity. The golden cross covered with diamonds and gems in the middle of the hourglass represents the time and the truth. Five groups of dolphins represent five groups of people responding differently to the truth. One group swims away from it. The next one looks for the truth in the wrong place. The third group is distracting others from finding the truth. The fourth group is being distracted and becomes the deceived spectators. The last group is bravely reaching right for the very truth at the bottom.

AKIANE

The Dreams • AGE 10 (acrylic on canvas; 48" x 60")

AKIANE

The five-inch figure grew to be a two-foot nineteen-year-old Jesus on my five-foot-long canvas. Every week He grew bigger and bigger—maybe just like the dreams He had. I repainted and repainted. Even though it took me three months and almost three hundred hours to complete it, and during this time I was very sick, busy, or traveling to art shows, the inspiration was very strong, and I could not wait to see how the finished piece would look after so many weeks of creating and waiting.

Only after I was finished God did tell me that He'd directed me to paint a few of the past, present, and future empires: the tower of Babylon with its highly advanced technology spheres building the tallest structure in the world, the Roman and Greek Empires, gold pyramids, buildings from Asia, and the tower in Russia without the star for fallen Communism. The Statue of Liberty stands as the symbol of the dream for many nations to live peacefully together, and the atomic sculpture shows how God recently opened the understanding of science and medicine. I don't know what the river and many other things I painted mean, but everything turns out to symbolize something important. A puzzling thing happened about one year after I painted this painting. I received the news from scholars and archeologists that their excavations showed the Tower of Babel being called a tower of spheres. It never ceases to amaze me how God uses my hands.

The meaning of this painting is that God is in control of all time and of all dreams. I painted Jesus as a joyful young man because He can see the great future, even though we might not. His dream is that we all love God and one another. Dreams are important—they are the doors to faith. The orange is the color of listening, and Jesus calls us to listen to what He and His Father in heaven have to reveal to us all.

By the Moonlight • AGE 10 (acrylic on canvas; 16" x 20")

The triumph of joy over suffering is the story of this painting. A few of my paintings are like gessoed-down motion pictures where I paint the beginning and the middle of the story, but paint over them, leaving only the end to be seen. Just like this one, where at first I painted the egret with its neck down and sad. Then I decided to lift its head up so it would face life bravely.

AKIANE

Butterfly Passion • AGE 10 (acrylic on canvas; 48" x 48")

Whether in his dream or for real, downstream a horse is running after his love, while the love butterflies surround him. The bubbles represent womb and beginning. As soon as the two horses meet, the bubbles will burst, releasing the butterflies. I painted this scene to express the search for love and its meaning.

AKIANE

The Challenge · AGE 10 (acrylic on canvas; 36" x 48")

The challenge of the choices is the maze. The light is ahead for the journey to continue safely. But because of hunger, exhaustion, the cold, and the shadows, the horse is losing its focus. The blue is the color of the mind; therefore, I painted the shadows blue to create a mental challenge and confusion. The challenge for the tired horse is which direction to choose. This is an allegory about our choices.

AKIANE

The Forbidden Fruit • AGE 10 (acrylic on canvas; 18" x 20")

One morning I woke up earlier than usual, and right away I decided to paint—but I could not find any canvas in my studio. My family was still asleep, so quietly, still in my nightgown, I searched my art closets and found one small canvas that I'd worked on a few years ago, but later gessoed in black. After my prayer I began painting a young woman's portrait next to a branch of fruit. Suddenly I felt God say, Blend all the races, because this is Eve, the mother of all mankind. Right then and there, I understood the meaning. The tree of the knowledge of good and evil is full of forbidden fruit—red for the knowledge of evil, and green for the knowledge of good. It was created to be tempting, fragrant, and easy to be picked. Although the fruit resembled grapes, it wasn't. At first, Eve thinks that she will gain wisdom by biting into the fruit of knowledge, but unexpectedly she finds the deception as the red blood of suffering drips from the green fruit. The knowledge of good and evil is simply too much for a human to understand and experience, and now Eve is looking up to God for forgiveness and help.

AKIANE

The Pyramids · AGE 10 (acrylic on canvas; 36" x 48")

In one of my dreams, I saw the image of white pyramids beaten by the ocean waves and surrounded by live bubbles. Unlike most of my paintings, I had no idea what those symbols meant, but I painted them anyway. Today the meaning still remains a puzzle.

AKIANE

Hope · AGE 10 (acrylic on canvas; 48" x 60")

This is the second part of the story of the abandoned Asian girl that I first painted when I was nine. After her long communion with God in the mute field, she was drawn to the hill of the blossoms, where she now rests in a golden dress and smells each fragrant branch. Behind her are foggy lakes, gray sky, gray mountains, and sad memories that she's left behind. But on the top of the hill there's a spirit of hope and love.

Akiane has been selected from more than one hundred of the world's most accomplished artists to create an original painting for the International LISTEN Campaign. Twenty artists have been invited to participate and lend their creative genius to support this unique global campaign to bring attention to the needs of children. This effort will benefit approximately two hundred children's charities around the world as it relates to war, poverty, aids, exploitation, and abuse. The six-month campaign will culminate in a concert event to be held at Madison Square Garden in New York and will be televised in sixty countries to more than five hundred million people, July 28-29, 2006. All proceeds from the sale of the original artwork at Christies Auction House (auction to be held July 30) will go to benefit the LISTEN Charity.

AKIANE

Angelic Love • AGE 11 (acrylic on canvas; 48" x 60")

Hair of pure gold. Veil of pure energy. Face of pure beauty. What the angel gazes at is of eternal significance. Yet what it is has not been revealed to me.

Akiane

Upside Down—Inside Out · AGE 11 (acrylic on canvas; 48" x 48")

I painted this as an allegory about purpose, balance and contentment. While some plants are content with who they are and where they are, many are not. Some are artificial plants, some are real, and others are artificially real. Then there are plants growing alone or dominating weaker ones. Still others are plain and peaceful. A few see life radically different while they live upside down. Other plants are used for decoration or simply being knocked down. Some wish to be outside experiencing more changes. Outside the window some plants long to be inside the house believing it is always safe and warm there. Yet all of us, just like plants, have different personalities and purposes. We need differences that unite us, not separate. But more than anything, we need light. Without light we will wither even in the most expensive and beautiful vases.

AKIANE

The Separation • AGE 11 (acrylic on canvas; 36" x 48")

So many children have been lost through war, famine, slavery, kidnapping, crime, disease, accidents, suicide, miscarriage, or abortion. When a child is gone, the only joy left is the memories and faith that we will see them again. And we will.

AKIANE

Co-Creating (self-portrait) · AGE 11 (acrylic on canvas; 48" x 60")

Right after my eleventh birthday, I visualized my self-portrait through the view of a canvas and through the eyes of the spirit.
I hoped to express the joy of co-creating, and the awe of feeling God's love and wisdom. My palate is the universe, and I dip into
the stars with my brush for colors.

AKIANE

akiane
her poetry

The Hollow Compasses

Our thirst is drying the distance
There are no longer silent streets
It is not our eyes that see God's love
Time watches us like naked seeds

The liars are timing the truth
With blisters trapped in the strife
When knives of conceit divide us
Who will find our forgotten life?

The doubt we paint is always a prison
The dried-up light escapes last hail
The darkness sheds its poisoned voices
With hollow compasses we sail

The Empathy

Confused by the first frost
the summer ends . . .
The hollies I picked
are voices of autumn
The wooden feet are limping
by the wooden fence . . .
When I have to run
I walk

Each

where Each corner of the earth
meets the edge of the sky
purring rain surprises young summer

as i touch every silver star
i glimpse a rainbow on me
Each mystery is an adventure

my feet touch a river
rolled to a scroll where Each wave
like a runner passes me a waterlily

Each day the sifted seeds
hear the pulse
of the sun yawn

Each branch
holds the hurricane
from running over me

choosing love
through the moss of the youth
Each limp is not felt like a lifetime

AKIANE

My Sight Cannot Wait for Me

I cannot stop holding my brush
On the blank canvas I sign
With blindfolded balance I paint my own eyes
Blue is the color of the mind

Do God's footprints follow His footsteps
Nobody hears what I see
We cannot trespass our Creator
My sight cannot wait for me

The Planted Eyes

God's love
is my painting
Silent mountains suffer in pride
As wild spring blends the time
my breath
searches heavenly mind

Blue wind
surrounds the sleepy lilacs
Each sound is a sacrifice
I can hear God's whitest whisper
Thorns have cut
my planted eyes

Many Lonely Paths

White roses of hope meet together
in the orchard of youth
Straight path escapes the winding roads
I leave home for the truth

The names I'll never know I can't forget
Is there someone to feel I'll never see
I cover a stranger with the first moment
and blades of ages start sweeping through me

Tension of battles keep wasting the truth
The wounded fall on its broken shoulders
The unfaithful faith can't keep its own trust
if priests still faint behind the soldiers

When there is no love to remember our lips
mirrors show up only at night
Cities with masks but faces still naked
The hands are wrapped in the sleeves of the fight

I'm chained in my own prophecies
The complaining glance again stings the past
I rescued my birth from the crowds
The light has many lonely paths

I cannot count how many lives I live
and how many times the salt meets the tears
Whenever the eyelids shut off the silence
eyes forget how to spin like the spheres

God's love will finish time
and the cross will be washed ashore
When He calls me to come home
cold swans will shiver by my door

AkIANE

The Footsteps of Spring

impressionistic footsteps of spring
catch and melt
each snowflake with its fingertips—springertips
and i find myself in a hoop
skipping over
a skiing breath

the eyes get lost inside volcanoes
painted on the linen canvas
with a brush made of marigolds
where I wake up with a long yawn
and where I go to sleep with the same long yawn

The Horse

as wildflowers stumble among the weeds
they fall asleep dreaming the whole spring

the pollen evaporates—
the laughs gush into a pail

an odd blinking eye
across the half of the head

from a laughter my throat fills up
with liquid ginger

Life Without a Leash

yesterday's promise is
today

when a storm arrives
is it the time
to nail a fence into our house
and strip a willow branch for a leash

only for you the fence is open

your laughing bark tugs my pride

in the cold twilight
you wait for me to sleep
and as we cuddle
we both sleepwalk

my bed is full of you

AKIANE

I Run—I Fall—I Dive—I See

Hiding in my own confession
I connect to another puzzle like me
When upside down I am unveiled by your grace
I run   I fall   I dive I see

Let me go to the top where dreams are born
Everything that is real or made up
Even when I am alone the time still passes
But when I am with you, the time just fills up

I feel a tangled piano wire inside
And a twin pebble sanded for disguise
I hold my own hand as a new friend
With a voice of love without a price

Your transparent skin reflects my gestures
As I find the weeds on a crown
And kneeling together we gnash like rocks
Just to make a surrendering sound

When wrongs hurt, indifferent trees bow down
To so many roads intertwined in a maze . . .
One of my eyelashes blinks without my permission—
Thinking of you I dive so many ways . . .

Wetness from my hair pulls a wagon
And each hair separately cries . . .
I break a vase with your wings
And with clay fragments the hair dries

Noticing one missing feather
I find every shade of white I still could be
So many ways you touch me
I run I fall   I dive I see

AKIANE

My Mother

I still remember five summers ago
Out of the train I tossed the seeds
Today azaleas surround the tracks
And railroad holds my mother's beads

How many lights are in her hands
How many hands are on her knees
How many knees are in her eyes
How many eyes are in her trees

From her quiet lips her prayers part
Her smile gets stuck onto my cheeks
The neighbors envy her warm kisses
Her house is full of running creeks

To feel the threshold of her face
I was invited to be born
I still remember still remember
The ignorance of that fresh morn

How thin is one hair, how thick is her braid
Her meekness speaks enough words in one glance
I love to share my silence with her
When I hold my mother's tender hands

I turn around and her weeping is love
In the cracked glass mortal thirst still dwells
How can her heart still more quietly beat
As her songs still wait for my turning bells

AKIANE

If the sheath is empty sorrow fills it up
How many worries hold her bandaged sores
Holes in the web are just her fingerprints
Her desire holds no chairs or doors

As summer fruit lands on the autumn snow
Her arms stretch out to carry me
As I fade away in her childhood dreams
I whisper to my brothers—let her sleep

The years passed by and I did not know
The carpenters who built our homes
While the whole flock slowly crowded her shoulders
On sidewalks I kept writing my poems

I call myself twice. But I do not come
My sight has blended with what she can't see
When streets step on sidewalks I wake her up
God wants to plant me like azalea seed

The first and the last time I saw my grandmother Aldona from Lithuania for a month was when I was four. I still remember her smile and the words she whispered to me: "I believed in God all my life, but I was afraid to share it with my family and friends. Don't repeat my mistake, Akiane. Share your faith with others. It will bring more happiness to you and to others. And never give up your passion." Although my grandma had lived through war, death, famine, and sickness, she never complained about anything. I once had a dream that she died standing and with a smile. This poem is dedicated to her.

My Grandmother

When I want to think like my grandmother
I need her cane. I need her cane.
When I want to see the flower planted by the tree
I need the rain. I need the rain.

When the porch can no longer hold her steps
I need to carry her. I need to carry her.
When the stiff nights no longer bow
I need to bury her. I need to bury her.

When the ladder is leaned against the swing
I need to climb. I need to climb.
When her wet crocheted tablecloth is wrung out
I need the time. I need the time.

When her coffin is filled with the skylarks
I need to swing her. I need to swing her.
When the icicles melt from her cane
I need her fingers. I need her fingers.

When the rest has no trust in the ground
I need to pray. I need to pray.
When the other side of her yard is a stream
I need God's bay. I need God's bay.

AKIANE

The Raking

Next to rabbit holes,
around the wind-kissed blossoms
summers are born to hatch eggs in the nest.
So many answers in pebbles alone!
So many caught fireflies in so many perfect minutes!
So many clear hours stretched along the shore to rest!

When summers prolong evenings,
creases of curtains stay openly white,
and I hear the trains.
Every time a train comes,
without noticing,
it passes the summer kite.

I am too slow watching grass.
The train has left. But there's another.
Perhaps through another century
it will take me
to find out who I am.
The autumn again is here to rake me.

The Dreamfence

kittens wait to jump into my dream
each time I visit heaven
they jump over a dreamfence

red clouds are ready for loving
as I love
my love paints my cats

our minds are somehow stuck together
as we dream together
of our own heaven

and after they curl up
inside my sweater
we knit our own heavens

AKIANE

Again I Find the Winter

I cannot find any reason
to be in the snow
where only bitten echoes are heard

Shadows of enriched colors
hold me
like ten-dimensional hands

Hopping on top
of each frostbitten grasshopper
I drill the hills

While kissing universes shed
a pearl nobly swells up
out of the borders of a shell

When trumpet eyes blow
a breath of desire
is so still

With sealed-up dust fading the prime
the handmade cast is molded
for eclipsed love

Looking for summer
in the falls of the spring
again I find the winter

It's Not Too Late

Perhaps I wanted to catch it
Perhaps not

But one morning
an eagle dropped a diamond
and right then with my faulty brush
full of my own hair
I wanted to paint

I wanted to paint
the wings—
Too late—they flew away
I wanted to paint a flower
Too late—it withered

That night the rain
was running after me
Each drop of rain showed God's face
His face was everywhere
On homes and on me

I wrung out the love to make the red
I wrung out the stumps to make the brown
I wrung out the trust to make the pink
I wrung out my own eyes to make the blue
I wrung out the seaweed to make the green

I wrung out the nightly pain to make the black
I wrung out my grandmother's hair to make the gray
I wrung out my visions to make the violet
I wrung out the truth to make the white

Today I want to paint God's face
IT'S NOT TOO LATE

AKIANE

The Anthill Ashes

When life lies down on the song of a bird
The resurrection returns my name
And I break the brakes of senses
To taste the steady pain

My cross is nailed into me
I pity the fingers that scourge my face
The minutes hurry the hours
The hours hurry the days

The loyal faces approach
And run along with every summer
Beside the flooded feet of love
The hardened lives are turning numb

Between my feet against the wind
My words will cascade through the strife
But if inside my eyes you see the flying geese
The ropes will pause the next worn life

The seasoned time has buried signs
And swings like a branch above a lost sandal
I step inside the anthill ashes
Becoming a new and larger anthill

The Antlers

How much silence at noon!
How much roar at night!
I still feel the trains blazing in me
and tracks following my footsteps.
I tried to get away. I tried.
It seems that my hoof is still stuck there . . .
where I felt my first snow inside . . .

Unwillingly my antlers kept on swinging in my red shadow
until that morning, when I smelled someone behind me, whom I loved.
I walked inside her with my love . . .
and her white rose eyes were stinging and closing my eyelids
like beehives.
She was the light that went through my path of self-pity.
Forgetting is remembering!
Every time I forgot, she remembered.
Every time she forgot, I remembered.

When she was thirsty I shared my thirst with her.
Every time I licked the bird off the branch,
it was a bare tree in winter.
Every time I looked at the clouds,
it was a love storm in summer.
Every time she raced me, her eyes were closed.
Every time I raced her, my eyes were opened.
Her smooth nose and my calloused nose
kept on rubbing against each other.
Our love was growing love.

Probably Christ climbed on our backs many times.
Together with eagles He was going in the future,
but we could not leave the fields
where in the hay so many songs we tasted.
Those days keep on returning to us,
as we grow old and as we see so many young antlers!

AKIANE

The Clematis Dream

Love was created to create . . .

Children enter a meadow and play hide and seek.
They run so fast that sunlight cannot catch them.
It looks as if they are hunting themselves.
Life seems longer when you jump in the grass. Without the reins.

My mother plants me on her favorite flower, the clematis.
The vines of clematis seem to be planted in the air.
Should we grow up like that?
The petals are closing and wrinkling from my breath.
Every petal or stamen I try to hold on to just falls out.

My brother is on the edge of a flower. He slips and falls down on the dirt.
It is so foggy no one sees him. Every time he moves, it becomes more foggy.
His muddy shoes in the fog do not look so muddy after all.
His raincoat is full of hail. The hailcoat.

I gather the fallen petals to celebrate
and planting a seed bigger than the whole garden I water for two.

Every time I walk, the strings fall out of my pockets
and I find my grandfather's letter beside his grave on a meadow.
On top there is a can, so every time I run over it, he would wake up.
My grandfather's white ring is on my finger.
It is always with me like a cast.

When I run, my eyes are closed,
and I bump into the childhood tree with a hammock full of the clematis pollen.
The hummingbirds land. They are to become the future.

That is all I remember from my dream.
I am only a child, but I remember everything I need.
Everything I know is someone. Everything I think is someone.

Love was created to create.

AKIANE

Faith

Covering voiceless sun the night cries out loudly
and wants me to braid the end
Together with nightingales' feathers
the eyeroots like unused candles bend

Battles on each of my hands
I am prepared to throw a shield
Stairs of remembrance so narrow I slip off
Finding an arrow I find myself in a mute field

How many stars do we have to own to feel wealthy
The blindfolded answers without question unwind
Let the lightning with salty emblems show the path
Tasting your tears inside your tear ducts I hide

But why to hide if no one is searching
When I sleep on the thawing snow
a thorn kisses its torn scars
and I pull out an old hair I do not own

Riddle verses on every forehead
I wake up at the beginning of a year to see
that without you I cannot be what I want to be
and without me I cannot be what you want me to be

AKIANE

Silence

With each silent lip
with each silent way
silence can also be mistaken

Sometimes dreams drop
like thousands of raindrops
from the very eye of the storm

While looking through my dream windows
strength passes by
fading the light

Stretched on the returning truth
each rest burns the brown bark
a browner shape of eclipse

And out of the ponds
cluttered with rain
half of the streams open

Sitting on the antlers of the spring
where each spike holds the spasms of the future
I wipe off wild feathers in the wind

With each silent lip
with each silent way
silence can also be mistaken

The Evening Swan

You need to cleanse
and silence your eyes
for dizzy prayer
bounces off a wall
All of your smile
lands on a silent swan
You need her love
to catch you when you fall

Brassy visions
count each and every stone
There are so many lives
in this lonely womb
When feelings are hungry
mirrors show different faces
The only evening the swan lands
she looks for you

AKIANE

The Dance of the Mind inside the White

Whenever the rain scatters
the scent of balloons
spring spreads like breadcrumbs
Tasting fragile fragments
a single breath breathes
and laurels lie between twin winners

Rolling down the hills of guessing
I grow a garden onto myself
but the roots start growing on me
only inside a stem
A round day becomes the eclipse
making me look like a haystack

As time climbs up a storm—
we cannot hear each other
Every noon points to a finger
so it might bend the night
so the stars might stare strangely at us
like diamond arrows

As soon
as the waves of the world shake
the rough sea charges at me
for the long devotions
and three waves
lie down on my forearms

Through the filtered souls
filling up the hearts
kindred prayers are welcomed
Which world searches for me
while a dew gently rolls down
a cobalt blue petal

AKIANE

The Journey

Walking through the poppy universe,
My fingers rattle the hourglass isles.
Where the time sings in the crossroads of hope
I am a brush painting for miles.

Every letter of the names I sit on
Just hangs on the family space tree.
Which knowledge lock should I pick,
As providence chisels a galaxy key?

Balancing myself on just one finger
At first I think that everything is white.
From universe to universe I jump alone
Just to find out that I am still a child.

The Light-Bearers

the breeding season
is long
past

the berries
fall
into the salmon river

the growl
across
a humid forest

the light from above
separates
the waterfalls

AKIANE

Bald

bald and indifferent events pass
dissolving hearing

i squeeze a tune from a bald piano
a cracked coffin

and pick up
my scratched laurels

yet still I do not know
where to turn

fishing on an old bridge
i view the city lights

there everyone is too busy
to see a bald eagle land and share his secrets

we talk until I fall asleep
on his back

i wake up awaking the eaglets
and make a nest for their warm and bald wings

The Freedom Horse

On the ebony sand
the ashes dig like shovels
Out of each round seed—a round plant
Out of each round hoof—a round water splash
The life of the copper mind
gets tarnished with each green inch of rain

Every year in the midst of heavy stones
there are cotton plants
A heavy gallop like a wall for miles
falls calling a bird
The neigh of a horse spins like a beak
Every wave is a short serenade

As boats crowd the rivers and lakes
the round logs beat against them
and the minds are mined
Only the free and wild stallion
cuddles and saddles the sand
without missing a grain

AKIANE

Tulilips

Turning away from home
an iceberg meets a child's cry.
Its motion is deeper
than any emotion!
The infant touch
washes the dense redwood trees
stretched in drowsiness.

Collapsing waterfall slips on a rock
breaking a flute.
It is too early for bubbles to come out of the rush!
Along the horizon
where the sky still looks iron hard,
the glass-like traffic leaves
the dreams of song landscapes alone.

On the way home
the rags on the road are passed by.
That is the same road that leads
to a broken maple next to an old sand castle.
The nestling holds each of mother's ocher feathers
sensing that beneath the pulse of mocking memory
is a journey pebble with a hole!

Turning like a pale chalk
he grips the ground
to hear
the alarm of the tulilips
and to hear
the blinking resurrection lie down
above the long arch of the roots . . .

Courage

Our hands
still
hold today's future . . .

I still see the mill
standing way on top of the island in the ocean
and feel the last chill from steadily rolling heavy wave . . .

Changes fold back the past folding the heart
reminding me where I lived
up high there on the tree with the nature's view . . .

where faith
immediately could see
and immediately could believe . . .

Making the slide from the charcoal paper of times
I will tape my self-portrait
on a trumpeter swan . . .

Maybe she will explain my voice
writing for miles
for centuries and for choices . . .

Crossing the bridge
that is not even built
is courage . . .

Akiane

Found

Trading sap for water
we belong here.
Above the waterfall locks—our eyes.
Below them—our white diamond tear.

Around the cerulean blue nectar
our breath absorbs all the air.
We view what we ignore—
with mortal bows the stream appears so clear.

We bind the x-rayed light,
ignoring the escape of nothingness to clear the path.
For us, the barefoot orphans,
granite sandals are so hard to match.

The braided wax of hearing
crowns the lost smile to forgive,
and the shade of incense
stops at the edge of the cliff.

Losing the warbling life in a jungle,
our reflection drowns our washed emotion,
And, as the breeze paints the ripe births,
we receive the sense trained by its own motion.

Then suddenly without the mask or shield,
While our minds are conquered by the strange command,
we meet a friend we yield,
and leave in faith our jungle land.

The Summer Snow

Clouds move for miles
as I draw on them
with leftover grass
By the pond again I will sit
and wait for someone to pet me

Diving face down
off the cloud
and leaving each inch of white
I smell the aspen stumps
behind the shedding birch trees

Jumping from one air atom to another
and seeing myself
on top of myself
I breathe a different breath
I have never smelled before

Flipping over the earth pages
I go round and around
and it takes me forever
to find the white
in any other color

While the wind makes me breathe
I am like a flashlight in the light day
flashing the blankets
all tangled up into a braid
draped over fences

When I hum there now by the pond
rescuing the blossoms from the summer snow
I release a droplet of lukewarm water
stuck on my eyelids
Suddenly I feel someone petting me.

AKIANE

The Dreams (AGE 10)

The eternal road is the narrow road
where you wait for others to pass you.
As soon as the lungs of time
breathe camouflage that irritates truth
the centuries like dry branches fall one after another
breaking the masks, sphinxes
and artificial hearts of the empires.

The eternal road is the narrow road
where you wait for others to pass you.
The volcano crumbles the hideout of the last stage
and as the past applauds the future
the first-century waves roll over and over.
Is the dormant light still white
when the heaven gives birth to another earth
and the dew of the pangs drips all over you?

The eternal road is the narrow road
where you wait for others to pass you.
Why does a trillion-word dream exist if it cannot be opened?
Calling for the asking knots in the warm-blooded ropes
I lose my seamless robe
and the claws of rolling nightmares
slowly fade through the ripened dream in me.

The eternal road is the narrow road
where you wait for others to pass you.
On the worn
but still young crossroad of the wishes I leave love.
The resurrection of consciousness is faith!
Through the same faith you still
find yourself in a far future.

AkIANE

The Missing Years

With an oak mask the conscience hears
the acorns fall,
and all the hues of the rose break down.
Do you exist in the inanimate world,
if every raindrop shows no color,
not even white or clear?

You are the breathing survivor of spiritual perfection
in the sevenfold universe,
where the center of the wonder orb is shaken,
and I frame myself live,
sculpting out of myself the spiritual fabric
to dress up all of you.

At first the universe progress
feels like a statue of melancholic fog,
and only your breath can know,
how sore my throat is,
as it spits out a heart bubble,
where my clear eyes and woolen hair are seen.

Retiming your resurrected gaze,
I pass the future earth
to you,
so you could write my name on it
and pass it on to everyone
around this slippery world.

When clouds turn into puddles
for the children to walk on,
this is your chance to help the innocent.
Now you comprehend,
why the unstable sandals
are also on your hands.

AKIANE

Hope

The war in the soil.
The seeds are too young to fight.
While the eyes breathe
the guilty still feel no remorse.
The cobwebs with knots.

Across the blades of harvest
improper dreams wrinkle the childhood.
Without any cries
and without any touch
the cradles are left behind.

Bleeding
through hopeless unconsciousness
it seems that a rainbow gushes through me.
And rainbow-colored
I leak out onto the hope.

A silhouette of the eyes
follows me
to the warmth of times.
Only the innocence
grows the conception.

Held in dust
the pain of wisdom.
The trust is through hope.
Inside each fragrant branch
the colors of love . . .

AKIANE

By the Moonlight

The bowed beak
pierces through the skin of fire.
Kicking the world inside out
with deep blind worries
and harsh arguments
the filtered ashes
try to feel lonely,
but there is too much
of them.

On the ashes of a tree
only one ornament
is needed—
an egret
who by the moonlight
learns to cry
with all the questions
and to rejoice
with all the answers.

AKIANE

Butterfly Passion

Marching across the straining view,
saddles are on their own.
The pounding hooves like crushed bells
start suddenly to moan.

When I hold the armed love
controlling the courage in oak boats,
spoiled and regenerated sunbeams
cross the country raspberry roads.

Glittering landscape by the shores
is a newborn faith beaten by the countless waves.
Everything tempts me to love you.
Everywhere I run, love rains . . .

The revelation of the butterfly passion
in front and back throbs the same.
What a fresh smell of your eyelashes—
I braid them along with my mane!

In midsummer we are like two young angels,
inhaling love one motion at a time.
Your legs walk on mine, stepping on love,
and right away I sense the meaning of life.

To be born together, yet years apart,
we both rush out of the womb.
My eyes are blurry, yours are so clear
when I carry the river to you.

Your tears are free,
but mine are armed from above.
Let me hold our courage,
so the courage could arm our love!

AKIANE

Acknowledgments

My BIGGEST THANKS go to my family, who believed and supported my dream. Without my mother's loving patience and encouragement; my father's humor, energy, and loyalty; my older brothers' devotion and attention to the family's daily needs; my youngest brother's sensitivity and imagination; and my angels' selfless guidance, I would not be where I am today, and this book would never have been written.

I have special thanks for the relatives, friends, and acquaintances who inspired our family the most through both hard and easy times. There were those who encouraged us to homeschool. There were those who helped us when we were penniless. There were those who were instrumental in our spiritual growth. There were those who appreciated my art and poetry. There were those who understood the reality of my visions, and those whose faith and optimism were infectious, carrying us through very turbulent times. There were those who motivated us to write the biography. There were those who offered us shelter in their huts or mansions. There were those whose prayers brought miracles. There were those who shared our everyday lives, helping us to grow: Johana Koeb, Aldona Blisntrubiene, Vladas Blinstrubas, Stanislava Simutiene and her entire family, Alfred Guscius, Renee and Brent Caudill and their family, Amber Spring and her family, Sandy Ross and her family, Caroline Faber, Natalie Camino, Charles and Lauren Bisbee, Bob and Rhonda Beckman, Sheila and Mark Hubert, Chris Leonard, Steve and Sandy Charbonneau, Ilana Goldman, Kay Drumright, Debbie Heil, Buffy, Mary Cunningham, Susan Badell, Moe Segal, Linda Czir, Bill Wigley, Sylvia Castle, Dawn and Ross Radandt, Paul Keith Davis, Michael Lloyd, Susan Miller, Mirian Trobridge, Dubrava Pochernikova, Marina Koledintseva, Mathew Block, Ernest Moyer, Roger Jellinek, Rolla St. Patrick's School, and many others.

I also want to thank all the art students I've taught, wonderfully patient models who modeled for me, churches, galleries, and museums that invited me, photographers, cameramen, and media who allowed me to share my dream with others, fans who supported me with their letters, gifts, and smiles, many charities, especially the LISTEN campaign, Free the Kids, and Northwest Medical Teams for giving me an opportunity to help sick and poor children around the world.

My thanks go to all art collectors, but especially Brian and Susan Conrad, Steve and Abby Appelt, Sylvia and Richard Witt, Emory Miller, Holly and Daryl Robertson, Margaret Mills, Jerry Fuhs, and Whitey and Fran Menching.

AKIANE

I also want to thank those who were the most supportive and helpful in bringing my art and poetry to millions of people: Debbie Wickwire (acquisitions editor, W Publishing), Chris and Linda Gibbs (the reproduction printer), Karl Knelson (webmaster), Victoria Nesnick (president, Kids Hall of Fame), Emily O'Donnel (reporter, *Time* magazine), Paul Keith Davis (the speaker), Rick Hankock (ABI), Oprah Winfrey and her producers (*Oprah*), Robert Schuller (*Hour of Power*), Marjorie Neufeld (Miracle Channel/Life Line), Patricia King (Extreme Prophetic), Alyson Marino and Craig Ferguson (*Late Late Show*), Gary Dini (FOX magazine), Wayne Brady (comedian, host, *Wayne Brady Show*), Lou Dobbs (CNN), producers at *Good Morning, America* and *World News Tonight*. Many thanks to all television and radio stations, magazines, and newspapers around the world who shared my story and God's love.

Akiane

Index

(Artwork titles appear in italics; poetry titles appear in quotes.)

Testimonials for Akiane

"Akiane is a gifted and seasoned artist who is totally focused on her work. She is a renowned prodigy in the arts world!"

WORLD NEWS TONIGHT, ABC

"We have been collecting the paintings by Salvador Dali, Picasso, Marc Chagall, Miro, and now—Akiane!!!"

STEVE AND ABBY APPELT, Art collectors
United States

"To say that Akiane has extraordinary talent is a gross understatement. She is a young genius and a spiritual young lady with an amazing gift who is changing the lives of all who have come into contact with her."

FOX MAGAZINE/FOX NEWS

"Nothing has prepared us for this nine-year-old who has mastered the art of realist painting."

LOU DOBBS SHOW
CNN

"I see Akiane's paintings or read her poetry and it's very clear to me that God is with us, and He's close by. So very clear."

MICHAEL LLOYD
An Award-Winning Music Producer and Composer

"We believe Akiane's paintings were not merely divinely inspired, but divinely commissioned! We are honored and blessed to be the caretakers of "The Light Bearers." Their story is our own journey of faith. Akiane is fearless on the canvas. This painting is a beautiful expression of the Father's love."

SUSAN AND BRIAN CONRAD
Art Collectors, Canada

"Akiane is a sign of the times. What an incredible artist and poet!"

LIFELINE/MIRACLE CHANNEL, Canada

"What an amazing and talented young girl!!!"

CRAIG FERGUSON, *The Late Late Show*

"Akiane, you are an incredible young lady! We thank you for using these precious little hands to do incredible work for God. Absolutely spectacular paintings! God loves you and so do we."

ROBERT SCHULLER, *Hour of Power*, Crystal Cathedral
Garden Grove, California

"Akiane's innocence, her vision, passion, and compassion all come through in her paintings and poetry. I believe this young and gifted artist is destined to leave her mark in the world of art."

EDWARD SOLOMON
Co-Founder and Director of the International Museum of 21st Century Art
(TIMOTCA), Art Beyond Borders
Laguna Beach, California

"Akiane is a beautiful name in itself. However, you have to meet this ten-year-old artistic prodigy in person to see her beauty and the beauty of her art to appreciate her phenomenal talent! My wife and I have recently had the privilege of going to her home in Idaho and meeting the young lady and her lovely family. To say the least, we were astounded! To see her realistic paintings first-hand and to encounter her simple demeanor was the thrill of a lifetime!"

H.E. WHITEY MENSCHING
Collector and Assistant Curator, The Museum of Religious Arts
Logan, Iowa

"Akiane's strikingly realistic paintings, drawings and poetry are windows into the soul of her subjects, reaching a depth far beyond her years. Her captivating works create a powerful and lasting impression, rivaling the works of many adult artists. Akiane's unique achievements have earned her an induction into The Kids Hall of Fame."

VICTORIA NESNICK, PH.D.
Founder, President and Publisher, The Kids Hall of Fame

"Akiane is unique. She is a phenomenon. I have never seen an artist with such a unique gift as this young lady has, with absolutely no training at all. She produces some of the finest works of art I've ever seen."

MICHAEL O'MAHONY
President and CEO, Wentworth Galleries

"It seems that these expressions are not those of a young girl but of a mature poet whose aphoristic and enigmatic thinking come to her instantly. Hers is definitely a philosophical poetry, and our world literature can be so proud of this new *wunderkind* genius."

ALFRED GUSHCHIUS
Renowned Lithuanian Literary Critic and Poet

"Akiane is a literary phenomenon in the history of poetic art. I doubt there has ever been a literary child genius of such maturity, lyrical virtuosity, and spiritual transcendence! Her rare gift will be engraved forever in the history pages of the world's literature. I see the cosmic hope and meaning of life in her wisdom-saturated imagery. I am speechless!"

VLADISLOVAS BLINSTRUBAS
Distinguished Lithuanian Poet

"I have never encountered such talent for painting in anyone so young. Akiane's poetry is even more impressive than her painting. Her images are astonishingly mature and original: fearless, deep, and mysteriously powerful. Yet Akiane herself remains an unpretentious, unselfconscious, delightfully unaffected and playful ten-year-old girl!"

ROGER JELLINEK
Literary Agent and Editor

"Akiane is an absolute artistic prodigy! Her creation electrifies with the realism, the artistic sense, and the level of mastery, spectacular even for an adult artist. When I was first acquainted with the petite Akiane she was only five, and even then she amazed everyone with her abilities. I still to this day treasure the pencil sketches, including my portrait and a squirrel—live as live can be—that she gave me as a gift."

MARINA KOLEDINTSEVA, PH.D.
Professor, University of Missouri

"Fantastic works! I was impressed by her flowers. They are absolutely real and full of childhood soul. Without any argument or doubt, Akiane is great!"

VICTOR DEPUEV
The Academy of Sciences of Russia, Moscow

"We have known Akiane and her family for several years, since she was four years old, enjoying a close and rewarding relationship which we have been thankful for. To us she always seemed like a normal, happy little girl, apart from her very advanced and beautiful works displayed at home in Missouri, and a strong interest in spiritual things uncommon for a child."

RENEE AND BRENT CAUDIL, M.D.

"My wife and I have always been in awe of the talent that comes from just the slightest stroke of a brush and the thoughts of an inspired and truly gifted artist, but no other has touched and captured our family's heart, soul, and imagination more than that of Akiane. Not only is she a rare diamond artistically (an understatement), but most importantly she's a sweet angelic little girl who has the heart and ability to touch the world for the less fortunate, and through her hands, make it a truly better place. For this reason, her gift is invaluable and long awaited."

MICHAEL WARD, M.ED., Psychotherapist
EMILY WARD, CEO and President,
Le Triomphe, Inc. Intl

"I observed Akiane at school in Colorado and I knew her also as a personal friend. A precocious seven-year-old with an enthusiasm for living, she was a beautiful child with a strong faith in God already evident in her young life. I enjoyed watching her romp and laugh with their family's golden retriever in her yard at home. She had a unique art ability already displayed in her paintings at such a young age! She has truly grown into a self-motivated, talented young woman with the same attributes I observed in her as a young girl. Akiane's zest for living and her sense of humor make her a delightful individual.I see so much faith through her unique paintings. It has been a true pleasure to know Akiane. I thank God for showering His gifts on someone who will share them with the world."

SYLVIA CASTLE, M.ED.
Teacher

"Akiane's use of color, balance and execution are usually reserved for masters three to four times her senior. Her genius is her ability to absorb the world around her and translate exactly what she sees in perfect form."

RICK HANCOCK,
President/CEO, ABI, Art Dealer and Publisher

For more information about Akiane,

her art and writings,

see **www.artakiane.com**

or call 1-800-318-0947.